La Purísima Concepción

La Purísima Concepción

The Enduring History of a California Mission

◆ MICHAEL R. HARDWICK ◆

THE
History
PRESS

Published by The History Press
Charleston, SC 29403
www.historypress.net

Front cover, top: Etching by Ed Borein. *Courtesy of Santa Bárbara Mission Archive-Library.*
Front cover, bottom: Painting of La Purísima in the late 1880s by Edward Deakin. *Courtesy of Santa Bárbara Mission Archive-Library.*
Back cover, bottom: *Standing, left to right*: L. Deming Tilton, director, Santa Barbara County Planning Commission; Ronald L. Adam, SB County supervisor; E.D. Rowe, NPS landscape foreman; Frank E. Dunne, SB County forester; Harry Buckman, SB County Board of Forestry; Frederick C. Hageman, NPS architectural foreman; Arthur L. Darsie, NPS engineering foreman. *Lower row, left to right*: Wallace C. Penfield, SB County Planning Commission engineer; Lawrence Libeu, NPS fire suppression foreman; Arthur Woodward, archaeologist, LA County Museum; H.V. Johnston, NPS camp superintendent; Dr. Owen C. Coy, director of California State Historical Commission and chairman of Department of History, University of Southern California. Restoration policy meeting at La Purísima, August 1934. *Photo from An Archeological and Restoration Study of Mission La Purísima Concepción, Reports Written for the National Park Service, by Fred C. Hageman and Russell C. Ewing, edited by Richard S. Whitehead, 1980.*

First published 2015

ISBN 978.1.5402.1394.5

Library of Congress Control Number: 2015933531

CONTENTS

Foreword, by Jarrell C. Jackman, PhD   7
Preface   9
Acknowledgements   11

1. Missions as Frontier Settlements   13
2. Spanish Beginnings in the Lompoc Valley   17
3. Chumash of the La Purísima Area   24
4. The Founding of La Purísima Concepción   35
5. Neophytes and Franciscans   44
6. Economics of the Mission   52
7. Ranches, Lands and Roads of La Purísima   57
8. Indian Life at the Mission   62
9. Indian Revolt at the Channel Missions   69
10. Secularization of Mission La Purísima   82
11. La Purísima Mission Garden   88
12. Restoration of Mission La Purísima   92

Glossary   97
Appendix 1. Timeline of Building Construction at
    La Purísima Mission   105
Appendix 2. Escolta (Soldier Guard) Assigned to
    Mission La Purísima   111
Appendix 3. Significant Indian Villages of the La Purísima Area   115

Contents

Appendix 4. Cultivated Crops Grown at Mission La Purísima   121

Appendix 5. Sources of Plants for Restoration of
   Mission La Purísima   123

Chapter Sources   127

Bibliography   131

Index   137

About the Author   143

FOREWORD

Michael Hardwick has produced an important new, long overdue history of Mission La Purísima. It has surprising depth and breadth—it provides a good background introduction of the Indian (Chumash) peoples who lived in the area of the mission and who became the focus of the padres' efforts to teach European agricultural practices and crafts; we are also introduced to all the padres who served at La Purísima through short biographies and learn of their efforts to convert the Indians to Christianity. We learn, too, of the first mission that was destroyed by an earthquake in 1812 and relocated across the Santa Ynez River.

We experience in this history the vastness of the mission lands that spread across thousands of acres and were covered with orchards, fields of wheat and other grains, not to mention the thousands of cattle and sheep that were introduced as well. This had a huge impact on the traditional life ways of the Indians, who were really left with two options: join the mission or disappear as a people. The rural agricultural and livestock world of the Lompoc Valley and the surrounding area created during the mission period has survived to this day.

This volume also provides a detailed account of the Chumash revolt of 1824 that started at Mission Santa Inés and spread to La Purísima, and lastly, we learn of the noble efforts of the Civilian Conservation Corps to restore the mission in the 1930s that would eventuate in one of the crown jewels of the State Park System—La Purísima Mission State Historic Park.

The 225 years covered in this history contain many factual nuggets that jump out, such as the mission producing more than forty thousand wool blankets during its years of operation. Because of their European origins, the padres were familiar with the wool industry, which sustained the Spanish economy during this time period. No wonder, then, that there were more sheep at many of the missions, including La Purísima, than cattle and horses. No wonder, too, that some of the building practices used in Spain and inherited from the Romans—such as enclosed quadrangles and aqueduct systems—became now well-known features of these treasured mission sites along El Camino Real.

Speaking of El Camino Real, there has been a movement afoot in recent years to designate El Camino Real in both Alta and Baja California as a World Heritage Site. To achieve this status, more thorough research of each mission site and other colonial and Mexican sites—such as this volume has undertaken of Mission La Purísima—will be needed. One can hope that such studies will follow. For the moment, we can take great pleasure and draw insights from the fruits of Michael Hardwick's labor. It has clearly been a labor of love, as indicated by his personal involvement with the mission in the early years of his career. It should be read widely by all interested in the history of the California missions and by students of history seeking to understand the European colonization that laid the foundation of the California we live in today.

Jarrell C. Jackman, PhD
Executive Director
Santa Barbara Trust for Historic Preservation

PREFACE

L a Purísima in two centuries went from a fledgling frontier mission to a State Historic Park. Unlike other California missions, La Purísima reinvented itself after major setbacks. Originally founded in 1787, the first mission grew around a quadrangle. The first mission complex was located in the town of what is now Lompoc. La Purísima Concepción grew to influence more than 1,500 Native Americans. A great Southern California earthquake in 1812 abruptly ended that settlement. A new mission was subsequently built across the Santa Ynez River in 1813, without a quadrangle and with an eye toward future destructive California earthquakes. La Purísima became the seat of California mission government from 1815 to 1823. Indian neophytes at the mission revolted in 1824. Following this, the mission fell into disarray after California missions were secularized.

In 1934, La Purísima reemerged from ruins. It was re-created as the result of a huge public works project under the auspices of the Civilian Conservation Corps. On the eve of the 154th anniversary of its original founding, La Purísima was ceremoniously opened to the public as a state historic monument. The date was December 7, 1941—the day the Japanese attacked Pearl Harbor and the United States entered World War II.

Since its opening to the public in 1941, the mission site and restored buildings have been maintained, protected and kept open to the public by the State of California. It became a State Historic Park in 1963. Over the years, the park area has been enlarged to include some vital parts of the original mission water system. The park system has served to protect the site

A contemporary view of the front of Mission La Purísima today. *Photo from the Jon B. Lovelace Collection of California Photographs in Carol M. Highsmith's America Project. Library of Congress, Prints and Photographs Division.*

from commercial and residential development that would have disrupted the pastoral quality of La Purísima's natural setting in *La Cañada de los Berros* (the canyon of the watercress).

In 1973, mission docents (*prelado de los tesoros*) began the interpretation of mission daily life. Today, with nearly one hundred mission docents, Mission La Purísima is being interpreted to more than fifteen thousand schoolchildren a year.

La Purísima Concepción: The Enduring History of a California Mission is the story about a mission dedicated to the virgin mother of Christ that refused to die in the face of radical change. The mission has been called the "Williamsburg of the West."

Acknowledgements

Inspiration for this book dates from the early 1970s, when I was an interpretive specialist at La Purísima Mission State Historic Park. Jack Mason was the area manager of the mission at that time. He took it upon himself to sponsor a special project to organize and develop an archive at the mission. The work was funded partially from grants of the La Purísima Mission Citizens Advisory Committee.

Numerous seasonal employees researched collections, contributed to seasonal reports and documented the living museum concept at the mission. Ursula H. Petty, Jacqueline A. Ball, Mary Rivaldi, Karen L. Wicks and S. Kristina Wilkinson assisted with the various projects. Kristina Wilkinson contacted the Santa Barbara Historical Society and convinced it to dedicate an issue of its journal, *Noticias,* to "The Founding of Mission La Purísima Concepción." This appeared in the spring of 1975. Historical artist Russell Antonio Ruiz illustrated the journal with very excellent drawings. Kristina now teaches Indian ethnic studies at Santa Barbara City College and is the museum director at Mission Santa Bárbara. She advised on La Purísima Mission art that appears in this volume and reviewed material included in the book on the Chumash Indians. Many thanks also go to John Johnson, PhD, of the Santa Barbara Museum of Natural History, who also advised on Chumash mission history.

Paula Hardwick, my late wife, spent long hours with me at La Purísima when I was doing my research. She first encouraged me to write and produce a book on the mission. My daughter, Patricia Hardwick, PhD in folklore and anthropology, reviewed the book and copyedited the text.

Russell Clay Ruiz graciously gave permission to use illustrations and paintings of his late father, Russell Antonio Ruiz. Many of these unsurpassed historical illustrations appear in this volume.

Dr. Jarrell C. Jackman of the Santa Barbara Trust for Historic Preservation was a great mentor and wrote the foreword to this book. Cheri Jasinski provided invaluable assistance in revising text and indexing the volume.

Chapter 1

MISSIONS AS FRONTIER SETTLEMENTS

Missions were colonial institutions of great importance in the spread of the Spanish Empire. Spain learned in the 250 years of its colonial adventure that missions offered the most economical means of settling a new territory. Lacking Spanish settlers, Spain used aborigines to colonize territories through the vehicle of a mission. A mission was relatively inexpensive to launch. It required one or two padres, a few soldiers and a quantity of supplies to establish. A mission became self-supporting soon after it was founded. Later, it served as a nucleus for permanent settlement. In California, twenty-one missions were founded between the years 1769 and 1823. Along with the missions, *presidios* (forts) and *pueblos* (towns) were the three major agencies used by Spanish officials to extend colonial borders and consolidate colonial territories. In California, the mission was the single most important colonizing agency. Four presidios were established in California as home bases for soldiers who served at the missions. Two agricultural pueblos (San Jose and Los Angeles) were founded in California to service the needs of secular settlement. Later, as the missions evolved, pueblos developed around mission communities.

California missions as frontier institutions were intended to be temporary. Legally, missions were allotted ten years to civilize natives sufficiently enough to run pueblos. A California mission under the Spanish system was considered to be an arm of the state. When a mission was started, it received a grant of $1,000 from the government. This was used to purchase bells, tools, seeds, vestments and other necessities

Missions Christianized and educated native Indians and called them neophytes. Initially, missionaries wanted to educate neophytes in their own language. California Indians, however, spoke twenty-five distinct languages between Sonoma and San Diego. Native vocabularies contained few words for things that could not be seen, heard, touched or tasted. As a result, missionaries often resorted to Spanish to teach native populations Christian doctrine.

Much emphasis was directed toward manual training. Each mission was a great industrial school. Neophytes were acculturated to a mission society by teaching them the skills of a trade or having them master the simple arts of agriculture. Training rarely got beyond industrial schooling. Mission compounds were hives of activity. Tanning, blacksmithing, winemaking, stock tending and the care of fields and crops occupied the men. Women learned to cook, sew, spin and weave.

Alta California missions conducted a flourishing commerce with trading vessels from the East Coast and foreign countries. By trading hides, tallow, grain, wine, brandy (*aguardiente*), olive oil and leatherwork, missionaries were able to acquire badly needed tools, furniture, glass, nails, hardware, cloth, chests, rendering pots, cooking utensils, lighting fixtures, musical instruments and a host of other items.

A typical California mission was a large rambling structure often formed around a square. Along the inner side of the square ranged an arcade, which served as an outdoor hallway connecting a series of rooms devoted to workshops, priests' quarters, dining and cooking facilities, storage and office space. The capstone of the quadrangle was always the church. Churches were beautifully decorated, often by the Indians themselves. Bell towers of the churches usually contained bells from Mexico or Peru that rang to summon neophytes to work or pray.

Franciscan missionaries attracted natives by offering them gifts of bright glass beads, clothing, blankets and food. Once the Indians consented to join a mission community, they had to get permission to stray from the mission.

Schooled in the basic skills of building and farming by artisans, neophytes were assigned to specialties in which they showed proficiency. Each neophyte was required to devote a specified number of hours per week to making adobe blocks or roof tiles, building walls, working in a handicraft or tilling the fields.

Franciscan missionaries were usually assigned in pairs to each mission. One friar was designated the superior. One watched over temporal and the other spiritual affairs, but friars frequently interchanged tasks. To relieve the monotonous round, missionaries encouraged the observance of nearly every feast day on their calendar; hence, processions, fiestas, games and celebrations were frequent occurrences. Neophytes were fed with three substantial meals a day, which freed them for the first time in their lives from the perpetual search for food that had been their preoccupation in pre-mission days. Many missions granted neophytes a two-week vacation every five weeks or so to visit their native villages.

Although the majority of the neophytes were content with their new way of life, many did not like regimented living. Some of the older men chafed under the restrictions of the daily mission grind, and they resisted it openly or covertly. The histories of individual missions are peppered with instances of runaways being hunted down and returned to the compound for discipline, usually a day or two in the stocks. There were also cases of large-scale revolts that resulted in setting fire to buildings, destroying crops or scattering herds. On the outskirts of nearly every mission lived unconverted Indians who sometimes harassed neophytes and encouraged the rebellious among them to escape.

To maintain order and return runaways, a corporal's guard (*escolta*) of five or six soldiers was assigned to each mission. In the case of Mission La Purísima, soldiers were detached from the presidio in Santa Bárbara. Soldiers moved their families to live with them at the mission and stayed in houses similar to those found in the presidio. The escolta provided protection for the padres, enforced authority among the neophytes and supervised harvesting and shop work.

Discipline was not wholly under control of the escolta. Padres appointed a small number of native police to assist in keeping order. Soldiers at the mission often trained Indian neophytes as *vaqueros*, or cowboys, and farmers. They, along with the padres, organized and trained mission Indians to act as a kind of militia. This became more important as the coast of California came under threat of war with foreign powers and attack by pirates. The militia augmented the ranks of the regular soldiers and assisted in emergency situations.

Wives of the soldiers were hired to teach methods of European cooking and housekeeping. It was not uncommon for soldiers and their wives to become godparents of newly baptized neophyte children. Some soldiers married Indian women. Often, children of the soldiers played together with Indian children and learned the Chumash language and native ways of doing things. At the close of the mission period, there were thirty-one thousand Christianized Indians peaceably existing within twenty-one missions under the control of sixty padres and three hundred soldiers.

The Mexican government finally secularized the California missions in 1833, and mission Indians lost the right to land that theoretically had been held in trust for them by the padres. Disenfranchised by social and political forces beyond their control, many mission Indians were able to sustain themselves in post-mission times by pursuing crafts and trades that they had learned at the missions.

Chapter 2

SPANISH BEGINNINGS IN THE LOMPOC VALLEY

The Lompoc Valley is a coastal valley that exists at the western edge of the Santa Bárbara Channel. It is situated immediately north of a promontory formed by Points Conception and Arguello twenty-five miles north of Point Conception. Point Conception (*Punta Concepcíon*) received its original name from the explorer Sebastián Vizcaíno when he first sighted the western extremity of the channel on December 8, 1602. This is the feast day of the Purísima Concepcíon in the Catholic calendar, referring to the Immaculate Conception of Mary, the Virgin Mother of Christ.

Hemmed in on three sides by rolling hills, the Lompoc Valley opens into the Pacific Ocean to the west. Close to the northern edge of the valley winds the Santa Ynez River. In the time before a dam controlled its flow, the river could be as wide as a mile as it wound its way to the sea. In the summer months, fog-laden winds blow up the valley. In the winter, rains pour down upon fertile farmlands, which extend eastward from the sea for more than ten miles before being hemmed in by the Santa Rita Hills.

The Lompoc Valley first became known to Spanish explorers when Captain Gaspar de Portolá and a handful of men made their historic journey from San Diego to Monterey in July–September 1769. On August 27, 1769, the expedition encountered a village, or *ranchería*, of 150 souls nearly one hundred yards from the sea, which was drained by a stream. Fray Juan Crespí, the diarist of the expedition, named the village *La Concepción de María Santísima* for the point on the sea behind the village as it had been named by Vizcaíno. In time, Crespí noted that a mission that would be established here would be given the same name. The explorers of the Portolá expedition camped at the mouth of the Santa Ynez River on August 30, 1769, and gave the names of San Bernardo and Santa Rosa to the river. According to Crespí, Chumash Indians were impressed with the Spanish, were very hospitable and made an effort to persuade one of the two priests who accompanied Portolá to remain with them. This was declined, and the expedition moved on to look for the bay of Monterey.

For eight years thereafter, the Spaniards gave little thought to the country of the Santa Rosa and its friendly inhabitants. In the spring of 1777, Father Junípero Serra proposed the building of three missions on the Santa Bárbara Channel "in order to make communications safer between the southern and northern missions." Before his death in 1784, Serra made his wishes known to Governor Felipe de Neve. Governor Neve approved of Serra's proposal to build the missions and used it as part of a plan to unify the province of Alta California.

In 1785, steps were finally taken for the founding of La Purísima Concepción. Sergeant Pablo Cota was detached from the escolta, or mission guard, of San Buenaventura to survey the Lompoc area for a new mission site. On June 2, Pedro Fages, then governor of California, recommended that the mission be established near the Santa Rosa (Santa Ynez) River for ease of irrigation. The site also offered adequate wood and pasturage for livestock. On March 24, 1786, Governor Fages was given approval to proceed.

Although Fages wanted to found La Purísima in the spring of 1787, December 8 was chosen for the dedication. December 8 was the feast day of the Immaculate Conception of the Virgin Mary. Father president of the California missions, Fray Fermín de Lasuén, performed the customary religious rites to found the mission in the presence of Governor Fages and a small group of soldiers and Indians. On the following day, Lasuén and Governor Fages retired to Santa Bárbara until the waters of the Santa Ynez River subsided.

So it was on a rainy December day in 1787 at a site called *Laxshakupi* by the local inhabitants and *Algascupi* by the Spanish that Mission La Purísima was founded. *Misión de la Purísima Concepción de la Santísima María* (Mission of the Conception of Most Holy Mary) was the eleventh mission founded in Alta California. It was located at the foot of the hills on the eastern edge of the flat fertile plane of the Río de Santa Rosa (now the Santa Ynez River). Fray Lasuén blessed the site and set a large cross into the ground to be venerated. He then celebrated the first Mass at the new mission, preached and recited

Portolá expedition, 1769. The expedition here is overlooking San Francisco Bay, but the scene could have been very similar at the mouth of the Santa Ynez River. *Painting by Lloyd Harting, from* The Call to California, *1968.*

A Chumash Indian ranchería very much like the one first encountered by Portolá in July–September 1769. *Drawing by Russell Antonio Ruiz, 1967.*

The founding of Mission La Purísima, 1787. *Drawing by Russell Antonio Ruiz, 1974.*

the Litany of All Saints invocation, a customary ritual when founding a new Roman Catholic church. The litany was recited to protect the new church and keep it from experiencing physical harm.

The founding missionaries at Mission La Purísima arrived in April, almost four months after the founding ceremony. They were Father Vicente Fustér and Father José Francisco Arroita. The first baptisms at the mission occurred on May 10, 1788. Three adult female Indians over thirty years of age were baptized with the names María Concepción, María Rosa and Ana María. By the end of the first year of the mission's existence, the fathers had entered ninety-five baptisms, twenty-five marriages and no deaths.

In a newspaper article written in the 1930s, a local resident recounted her experiences at the mission sometime prior to the turn of the century. She recalled many of the female Indians still left at the mission who all had the name María. Mary or María, of course, was the namesake of Mission La Purísima. Thus, the name of María continued to be commonly used for more than 140 years after the founding of the mission.

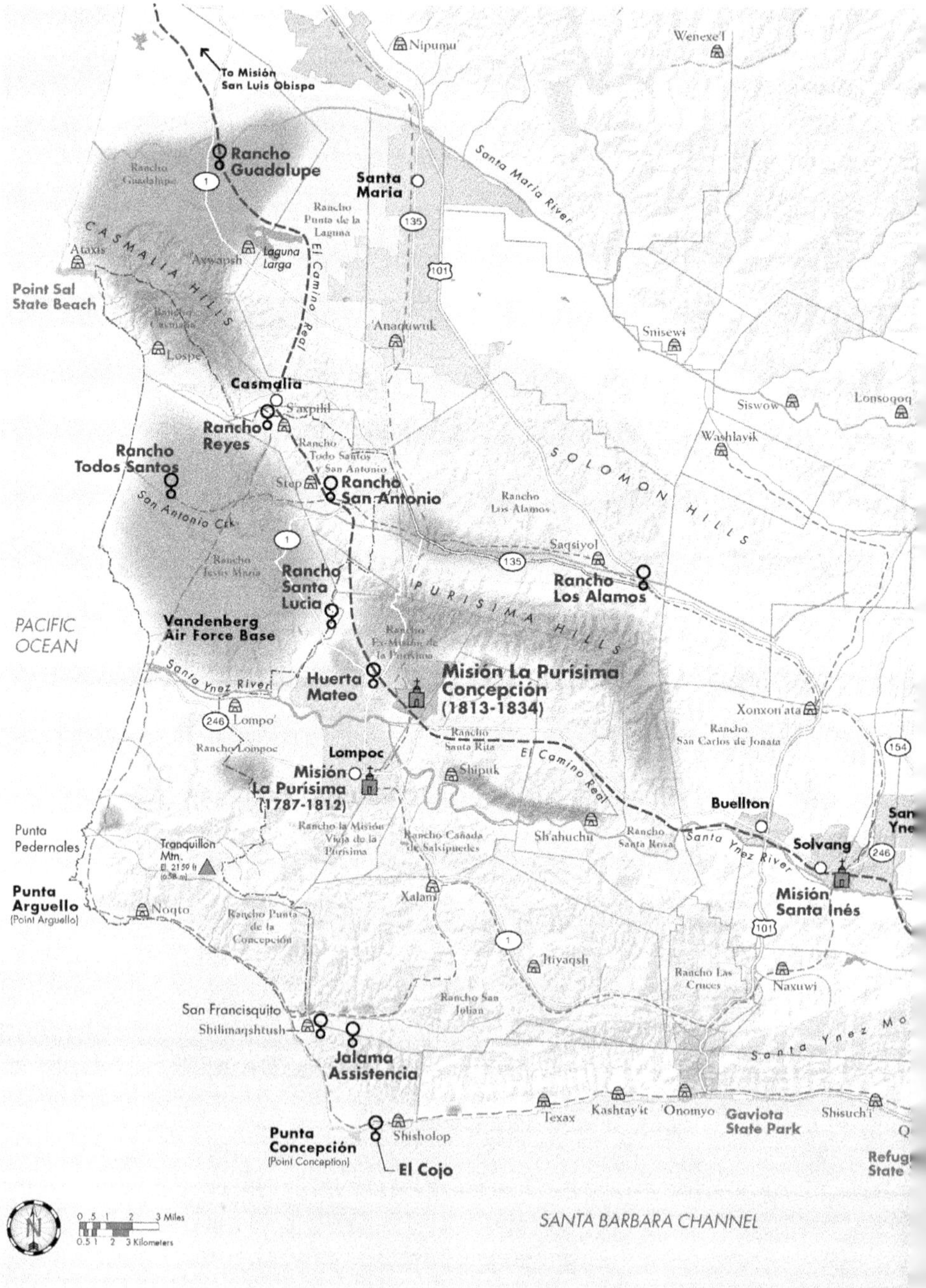
To Misión San Luis Obispo
Nipumu'
Wenexe'l
Rancho Guadalupe
Santa Maria
Santa Maria River
Rancho Punta de la Laguna
Casmalia Hills
Ataxis
Aywapsh
Laguna Larga
El Camino Real
Point Sal State Beach
Lospe
Anaquwuk
Snisewi
Casmalia
S'axpilil
Rancho Reyes
Siswow
Lonsoqoq
Washlayik
Rancho Todos Santos
Rancho Todo Santos y San Antonio
Step
Rancho San Antonio
Solomon Hills
San Antonio Crk
Rancho Los Alamos
Saqsiyol
Rancho Jesús María
Rancho Santa Lucia
Rancho Los Alamos
Purisima Hills
Pacific Ocean
Vandenberg Air Force Base
Santa Ynez River
Huerta Mateo
Misión La Purísima Concepción (1813-1834)
Lompo'
Xonxon'ata
Rancho San Carlos de Jonata
Rancho Lompoc
Lompoc
Rancho Santa Rita
Misión La Purísima (1787-1812)
Shipuk
El Camino Real
Buellton
Punta Pedernales
Rancho la Misión Vieja de la Purísima
Rancho Cañada de Salsipuedes
Sh'ahuchu
Rancho Santa Rosa
Santa Ynez River
Solvang
Tranquillon Mtn.
Misión Santa Inés
Punta Arguello
(Point Arguello)
Noqto
Rancho Punta de la Concepción
Xalam
Itiyaqsh
Rancho Las Cruces
Naxuwi
Rancho San Julian
San Francisquito
Shilimaqshtush
Jalama Assistencia
Santa Ynez Mo
Texax
Kashtay'it
'Onomyo
Gaviota State Park
Shisuch'i
Punta Concepción
(Point Conception)
Shisholop
El Cojo
Miles
Kilometers
SANTA BARBARA CHANNEL

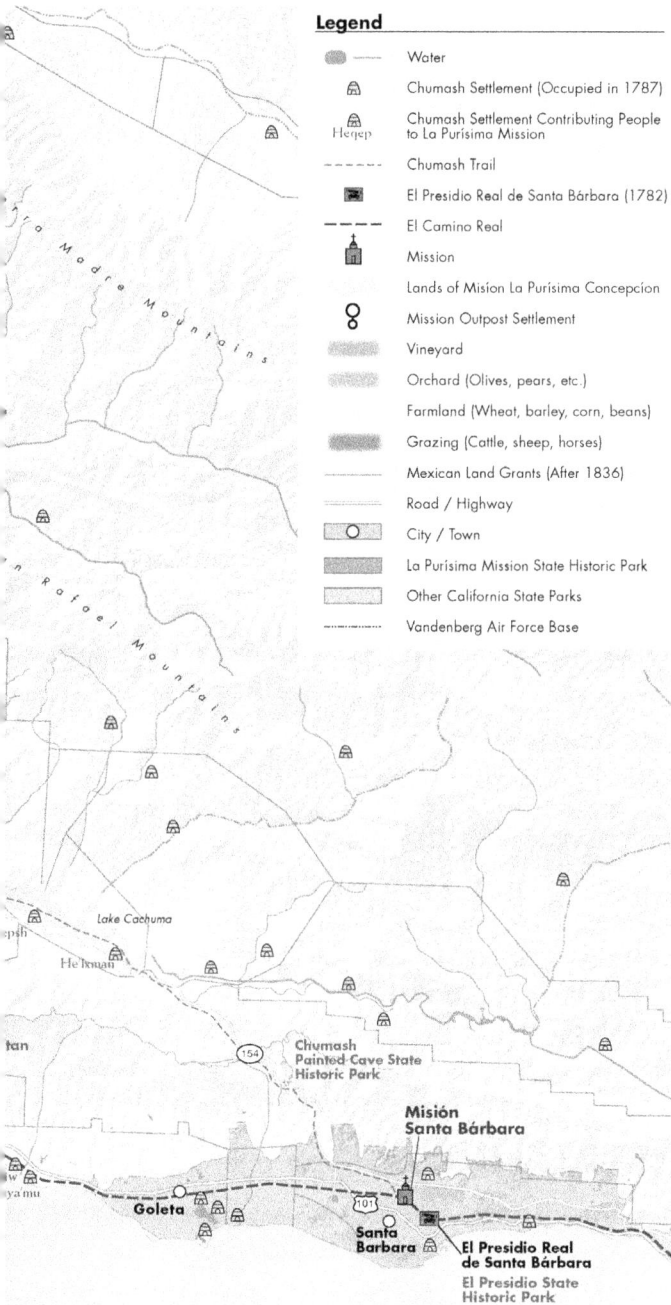

Legend

⬤ ----	Water	
🏠	Chumash Settlement (Occupied in 1787)	
🏠 Heqep	Chumash Settlement Contributing People to La Purísima Mission	
- - - - -	Chumash Trail	
▦	El Presidio Real de Santa Bárbara (1782)	
– – – –	El Camino Real	
🏛	Mission	
	Lands of Misíon La Purísima Concepcíon	
⚲	Mission Outpost Settlement	
	Vineyard	
	Orchard (Olives, pears, etc.)	
	Farmland (Wheat, barley, corn, beans)	
	Grazing (Cattle, sheep, horses)	
———	Mexican Land Grants (After 1836)	
————	Road / Highway	
▭◯	City / Town	
▤	La Purísima Mission State Historic Park	
▭	Other California State Parks	
············	Vandenberg Air Force Base	

A topographic map of the La Purísima area in relation to the coastline of California. Note the dotted line along the coast, which was the Portola route in 1769. *Courtesy of Channel Coast District of California State Parks.*

Chapter 3

CHUMASH OF THE
LA PURÍSIMA AREA

N ative Americans identified as Chumash are descendants of peoples who settled coastal California nearly eight thousand years ago. About one thousand years ago, native people from this region began to share similar tools, customs and beliefs. European explorers referred to them as *Canaliños*, meaning "a people who lived by the channel." The name Chumash comes from *Michumash*, or native inhabitants who lived on Santa Cruz and the Northern Channel Islands. The Michumash were known for their ability to make shell beads. Alfred Kroeber in his 1925 *Handbook of the Indians of California* coined the use of the generic name Chumash for people speaking Chumash-related languages.

Chumash peoples used shell beads as a form of currency. They essentially had a monetized market economy in which food, manufactured goods and some services were exchanged or purchased. Fiestas and other ceremonial occasions seem to have been important contexts for economic exchange.

Villages of the Chumash were located along the coast from Malibu north to the San Simeon area and inland as far as the western edges of the San Joaquin and Antelope Valleys. The three islands of Santa Cruz, Santa Rosa and San Miguel were also a part of Chumash territory. Estimates of population of Chumash peoples in historic times vary from eight thousand to more than twenty thousand, with fifteen thousand being the most reasonable number. The largest portion of this population was clustered along the shores of the Santa Bárbara Channel. There were at least six distinct Chumash languages. Five of the languages were named for the missions that were established in their areas. The documented languages of the Chumash are *Obispeño, Purismeño, Ineseño, Barbareño, Ventureño* and *Emigdiano. Emigdiano* is named for the San Emigdio area in northeastern Santa Bárbara and southern Kern Counties.

When the first Spanish land expeditions passed through Chumash territory in 1769, they found coastal villages of two to six hundred people. One village near the Goleta slough contained up to one thousand people. Villages of the coastal area of the Lompoc Valley were smaller. They tended to be located in the interior valleys, and only temporary camps were along the coast. Exceptions included the villages of Nocto, Pedernales (near Point Arguello), Shilimaqshtush or La Espada (at the mouth of Jalama Creek) and Lospe near Point Sal.

The area of influence of La Purísima went as far inland as Cuyama, north to Arroyo Grande and south to Dos Pueblos. Prior to the founding of La Purísima Mission, Chumash were trading with Indians in the San Joaquin Valley, and communication networks went far beyond that. Villages at Cojo/Shisholop (near Point Conception), Gaviota and Bulito/Kashtay't (near Gaviota) provided a large number of baptisms for Mission La Purísima. Chumash from the offshore islands were also listed in the mission records.

The Chumash lived in villages of varying sizes. Most settlements were on hillsides or hilltops overlooking rivers, streams or springs. Those located on the coast were often built next to sandy beaches. Villages had areas where people made stone tools, jewelry or canoes. Most settlements had a flat, smooth area that was used for sports. Each community had a special sacred area called a *siliyik* that was surrounded by tall walls made from reed mats. Colorful banners fluttered from the flagpoles that surrounded the siliyik. Throughout the settlement, the people set up various pole and thatch coverings for shade.

The social structure of a Chumash community provided a way of dividing people in groups and assigning them special jobs. Individuals were assigned to groups based on their sex, how old they were, how much wealth they had, what they did and who their parents were. The smallest social groups were families. Chumash families were combined into larger groups called clans. Clan members believed that their founder was an animal, such as a bear, an eagle or a coyote. Each clan was assigned a special job. Some clans had greater wealth and were thought to deserve special recognition. People of the most honored clans selected one of their members to be the village leader. The Chumash called this leader a *wot*, or chief. Women as well as men could be wots. Wots were aided by a number of specialists. The council

A typical coastal Chumash village. Note the plank canoes on the beach and flagpoles from which were flown colorful banners in the village proper. *Drawing by Russell Antonio Ruiz, 1972.*

of advisors, known as the *antap*, was one of the most powerful groups in the Chumash community. This group usually included the village doctors, religious singers, dancers and astrologers. Often, Chumash communities formed temporary alliances. Chiefs from the larger villages would gain control of several villages. These chiefs were called *paqwots*.

An average Chumash family lived in a small hut made from poles and bulrushes or reeds. The houses had circular floor plans and ranged from ten to twenty feet in diameter. In larger villages, circular houses could be up to fifty feet across. Houses were hemispherical, made by planting willows or other poles in a circle and bending and tying them together at the top. Other sticks extended across these, and to them was fastened a layer of mats or thatch.

In 1775, the viceroy of New Spain authorized Captain Juan Bautista de Anza to command an expedition to occupy and settle the port of San Francisco. The expedition originated in Arizona, crossed the Colorado River at Yuma and followed Indian trails of coastal California to its ultimate destination. Pedro Font, diarist for the expedition of 1775–76, described the

Left: Chumash Indian Raphael Solares near Mission Santa Inés wearing the ceremonial costume of a shaman. He was one of the last of the Chumash antaps. *Photo taken by French anthropologist Léon de Cessac, 1877, courtesy Musée de l'Homme, Paris.*

Below: Portrait shots of Chumash elder Raphael Solares without his ceremonial dress, circa 1877. *Photo by French anthropologist Léon de Cessac.*

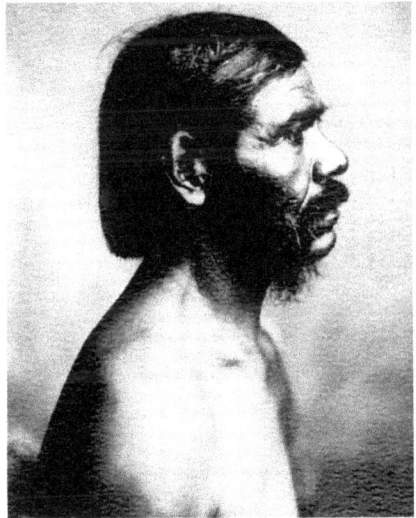

A Chumash jacal under construction showing the supporting structure beneath the tule thatch, La Purísima Mission State Historic Park. *Photo by author, 1973.*

numerous huts, or *jacales*, of the Santa Bárbara Indians. He found them to be very spacious, large and high. The center of the jacal had an opening to let out the smoke from a fire that was made in the middle of the hut. He observed that some of them even had window-like holes in the structure. Doors of the jacal were often barred with whalebone or sticks when residents were away.

A completed jacal Chumash dwelling. La Purísima State Historic Park. *Photo by author, 1973.*

Font also described village community playgrounds, cemeteries and sweathouses, or *temescals*. Near the villages were the cemeteries where Indians buried their dead. These were marked with poles and wood planks set upright in the ground. Poles held items that belonged to the deceased like baskets, shells, arrow bundles and other personal items. Ribs and other large bones of whales were used as grave markers.

Plank canoes, called *tomols* by the Chumash, particularly impressed Font. He observed that the launches were made by sewing together planks of wood using tools of "shell and flint." The boats were caulked with pitch or asphaltum and often decorated. The boats that Font saw were about thirty-six palms long and three palms across at the center. They were fishing boats and usually carried two Indians, one in front and one in back. Font was amazed at the quantity of fish that were caught by Chumash fishermen. He commented that when Anza first arrived at El Bulito Creek west of Gaviota, a launch had just come in that was loaded with "sardines." From this, Anza was able to purchase a supply of fish for his entire expedition and had to leave fish behind because there was no way to carry them.

This page: Chumash fishing from and rowing plank canoes. From a mural in Lompoc by Robert Thomas, 1992. *Photo by author.*

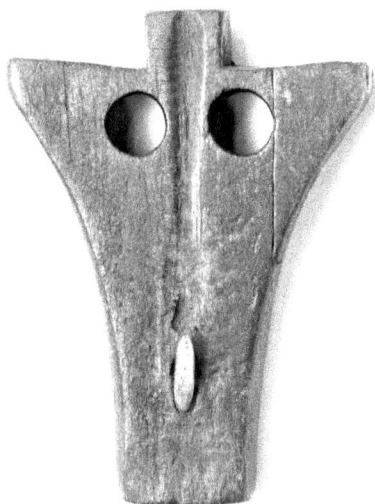

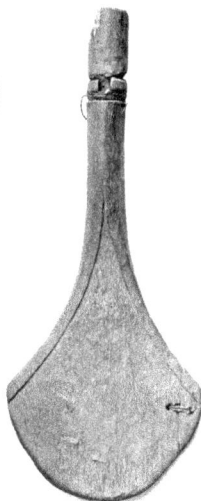

Far left: An atlatl throwing device. Chumash hunters or fishermen used this device to launch a spear with great force. Note the groove for the spear, the raised area that the spear butt rests against and the holes for fingers of the hand to grasp the object. The artifact was collected by Vancouver in 1793. *Courtesy of the British Museum.*

Left: A Chumash canoe (tomol) paddle blade collected by Vancouver in 1793. *Courtesy of the British Museum.*

Below: Side view of Chumash canoe paddle blade. *Courtesy of the British Museum.*

A TYPICAL PURÍSIMA VILLAGE

Purismeño territory was located in the ecological transition zone between central and Southern California. The major plant communities in this region are Coastal Strand, Coastal Sage Scrub, Valley Grassland, Foothill Woodland and Chaparral. The Purismeño used all the plant communities in their territory.

A typical Purismeño village was Shilimaqshtush, which the Spanish named Espada. It was located where Jalama County Park is today. Shilimaqshtush was a medium-sized village of between twenty and thirty houses, as noted by Portolá in 1769. At that time, he estimated that between 140 and 200 people lived in the village. Jalama Creek furnished a year-round supply of fresh water. Willows and tule—important for use in house construction and medicine—were found in the creek. The creek also contained steelhead salmon and trout. The most important foods for the village were acorns from oak trees, seeds (such as chia) and red maids from the grasslands and wild cherry, or *islay*. Dense stands of live oaks covered the slopes of the Santa

Ynez Mountains immediately inland from the village. Native seeds became especially abundant after fires. The fires were often set by the Chumash to produce crops of native seeds. Wild cherry and elderberries were scattered throughout the canyons and lower hillsides. Deer roamed the area. Tide pools near the ocean furnished limpets, barnacles, mussels and abalone. Seasonal camps were established to collect additional natural resources.

People who lived at Shilimaqshtush had kinship ties to people in villages throughout *Purismeño* territory. They were related to people living at Noqto near Point Arguello; Lompo´, the village of what is now the town of Lompoc; S'axpilil near Casmalia; and Lospe near Point Sal. Shilimaqshtush also had close ties to people living in villages outside Purismeño territory. Other locations with close ties were Mikiw (Dos Pueblos Canyon) in Barbareño territory and Tsikyiw, near Avila in Obispeño territory.

Mission records at La Purísima show that there was a great deal of illness at the village of Shilimaqshtush in March 1791. By 1796, only 12 people were living there, and 75 people from the village were living at the mission. In 1812, Shilimaqshtush had been abandoned. Mission records counted 101 people baptized from the former village.

As the Chumash came into the missions, they were offered a number of practical benefits by being baptized as neophytes. Spanish newcomers had ships, firearms, steel knives and tools. Spaniards introduced new

The village (or ranchería) Shilimaqshtush (or Espada), where Jalama County Park is now. This village was home to about 140 to 200 people in 1769 when Portolá first saw it. From a mural in Lompoc by Robert Thomas, 1992. *Photo by author, 2008.*

Cattle herds increased to take over native grasslands. Local natives were taught to be vaqueros (cowboys) to manage the livestock. *Artist unknown.*

Long-horned cattle became prized for their hides and tallow. Cattle herds grazed over the landscape, destroying aboriginal food sources, thus reinforcing the need for native Indians to move into the mission for food. *Photo from the Jon B. Lovelace Collection of California Photographs in Carol M. Highsmith's America Project. Library of Congress, Prints and Photographs Division.*

kinds of foods often produced by agriculture and the keeping of livestock. Agriculture provided relatively stable food supplies to mission Indians. Domestic animals like cattle, sheep, chickens, horses and mules improved transportation and also augmented food supplies. The Spanish also had many things of beauty, including paintings, statues, religious rituals and music. Chumash were also enticed by the preaching of the Franciscans. Often, whole villages moved to a mission led by the village wots. Wots and their families continued to serve in important leadership roles at the missions. The Franciscans and Spanish authorities assumed the role of chiefs, similar to the existing Chumash paqwots.

By the end of 1797, it was clear that the Chumash could no longer ignore Spanish settlement. Horses and cattle had multiplied and were disrupting the natural environment that provided sustenance for the Indian people. Chumash burning of fields to enhance native seed production was curtailed. Those who moved to the missions formed new mission communities and became known regionally by the mission where they resided. Chumash peoples took on Obispeño, Ineseño or Purismeño identities. Some traveled eastward into California's Central Valley.

Chapter 4

THE FOUNDING OF
LA PURÍSIMA CONCEPCIÓN

Founded on December 8, 1787, the first La Purísima Mission, or *Mission Vieja,* was the eleventh in the chain of twenty-one missions established by the Spanish in Alta California. Acting under orders from Governor Pedro Fages, Sergeant Pablo Antonio Cota traveled from Santa Bárbara to the Lompoc Valley in March 1788 with laborers and soldiers to construct the stockade and rooms necessary for the mission. The governor instructed Cota to be prepared to meet hostilities, to treat the Indians of the area well and not to arm them. Soldiers and servants were not to visit rancherías (villages of the Indians) unless ordered to do so. They were, however, to accompany missionaries when they visited the rancherías. Horse herds were to be guarded at all times, taking care that horses did not damage crops of the local Indians.

In a report to Governor Fages from Purísima in August 1788, Cota noted that he had marked off the mission square and had built a ravelin or bastion at the mission. Cota constructed the new mission on a plan similar to that of the presidio in Santa Bárbara. A ditch and defensive outworks protected the outer perimeter of the mission quadrangle so as to give protection against an attack of potentially hostile Indians.

Cota made surveys for good roads, and located the principal route, which connected Purísima with the northern and southern missions. In his August report to Governor Fages, Sergeant Cota mentioned that he had ordered Corporal Calluelas to take charge of a road called *Macario.* The road was easily repairable and was a shorter route to the mission. But it could not be

Mission Vieja de La Purísima was constructed in an enclosed quadrangle with defensive outworks protecting the mission. Outside the walls were Indian houses, or jacales. *Drawing by Russell Antonio Ruiz, 1974.*

Mission Vieja de La Purísima as it might have looked before the disastrous earthquake of 1812. Note the defensive quadrangle structures and the walled garden center right. Water reservoirs are visible at the center at the base of the large hill behind the mission complex. Near the reservoir on the left are the houses (jacales) of mission Indians living outside the mission compound. Based on research by Julia Costello, PhD, and Roy Salls, PhD. Artwork by Karen Foster, 1993. *Courtesy of the Lompoc Museum, Lompoc, California.*

used during the rainy season, as there were several ravines along the road that made travel dangerous. There is some speculation that this road may have passed through what is now the San Marcos Pass.

In August 1788, Sergeant Cota documented that there were five Spanish families at the mission and that he had sent for two more. He noted that mission residents already numbered seventy-nine Christians. In September 1788, Sergeant Cota finished his work at the new mission of La Purísima and was promoted from sergeant to *alférez* (ensign) of the presidio of Santa Bárbara.

In October, Alférez Cota reported to the governor that he had turned over the escolta of the new mission to Corporal José María Ortega and that he was detained at Purísima for eight days instructing the escolta in their new obligations. On December 31, 1788, Comandante Goicoechea of the Santa Bárbara Presidio reported to Governor Fages that the soldier detachment, or escolta, at La Purísima consisted of one corporal and fourteen privates.

MISSION VIEJA DE LA PURÍSIMA

The first permanent church of La Purísima was constructed in 1789 in what is now the town of Lompoc. It was made of adobe with a flat roof covered with straw and earth. It was about seventeen feet wide and sixty-two feet long. In 1795, Franciscan missionaries began to collect materials for a more permanent church. Foundations for the new church were laid in 1798. By that time, there were 920 Indians at the mission, and the existing church was not large enough to hold them all. Padres at the mission complained that they were compelled to lay foundations for the new church

A bell with an inscription that reads "La Purísima" is dated 1807. It could have easily hung in the first Mission La Purísima before the earthquake of 1812. The bell is currently in the Mission Santa Inés Museum in Solvang. *Photo by author, 2014.*

themselves without the aid of a master builder to guarantee the stability of the work. In 1803, the new church was completed.

Religious Art Adorning the Mission

By examining the religious art that adorned Mission Vieja de La Purísima, it is possible to form a visual picture of how the interior of the church might have appeared. Early Franciscan missionaries invested in religious art, which told a story, to attract converts. Before the earthquake of 1812, Mission Vieja had five statues, forty paintings and multiple crucifixes. Crucifixes were often used on side altars that were very likely in the church. In 1810, a *lienzo*, or painted-canvas wall hanging, adorned the front of the church. This was a backdrop for statuary. The lienzo was embellished with three carved niches (*nichos*) to frame statues that rested on shelves in front of the nichos. There were also eleven *colgaduras*, or cloth wall hangings, that were used as decoration. By 1804, twelve *cornucopias*, or mirrors with candle sconces attached, were added to the church.

In 1790, Mission Vieja received a small dressed figure of the Immaculate Conception, and in 1794, a canvas of St. John the Baptist arrived. The altar of the temporary church was first adorned with a painting of the Immaculate Conception. Later, in 1796, a large statue of the Immaculate Conception almost five feet tall was set in a niche in the wall above the altar. In 1798, a set of fourteen paintings of the Stations of the Cross was sent to the mission.

In 1801 and 1804, bills mention the shipping of twelve cornucopias. In 1806, the church received an *apostolado*, or a set of paintings of the apostles. Fourteen paintings in all, these would have been rather small oil paintings of Christ and the Virgin Mary along with the twelve apostles. In 1807, fathers at the mission requested seven large paintings that would hang in the new church at a height of about eight feet. The paintings were to be designed so that they would catch the attention and inspire devotion of neophytes at the mission. There is no evidence that these paintings were ever received, but among them were to be two large lunette paintings depicting the Nativity and the Burial of Christ. Painting themes included St. Joseph, Christ on the Cross, the Ascension of Christ in Heaven, St. Francis and St. Dominic.

In 1808, a request was sent to Mexico for a carved figure of the Risen Christ for use on Easter Sunday. This statue was to be two-thirds of a *vara* (2.8 feet) in height. Today, the statue is probably in the collection of Mission Santa Inés. In 1809, paintings of St. Anthony and St. Clare of about 5.0 feet in height were sent to La Purísima.

Left: A statue much like this of the Immaculate Conception was featured in the wall above the altar of the church of Mission Vieja de La Purísima. This particular statue is in the main church of Mission Santa Bárbara and is set in a niche behind the altar and to the left of it as you face the front of the church. *Photo by author, 2014.*

Below: A large lunette painting would have looked like this. Two such paintings hang in the Museum of Mission San Antonio de Padua in Jolon, California. The themes of the paintings that might have been at La Purísima do not match the themes of the lunettes at Mission San Antonio. *Photo by author, 2014.*

Earthquake Destroys Mission Vieja

An earthquake at Mission La Purísima on December 8, 1812, did little harm to structures. On December 21, 1812, at 10:30 a.m., however, the earth shook for four minutes so violently that it was difficult to stand. Church walls were thrown out of plumb. Another more violent shock came a half hour after the first, bringing down the church and nearly all the adobe buildings. According to accounts, various images and paintings were ruined, as were most of the mission furnishings. The most necessary items were dug out quickly. Heavy rains immediately followed the earthquake, burst the mission waterworks and made it difficult to recover buried items. Nearly one hundred neophyte houses were destroyed. Several neophytes were wounded, but none was killed. Small aftershocks continued for two days. At the time of the disaster, 999 Indians, 2 padres and a handful of soldiers resided at the mission. The mission was in essence a working ranch with 4,000 cattle, 12,000 sheep and 1,150 horses. It also had a walled orchard and vineyards. Mission agriculture produced wheat, corn and beans.

The earthquake that destroyed the mission at La Purísima was part of a series of earthquakes that damaged a number of missions along the Channel Coast and Northern Los Angeles County. Seven missions were damaged, some so severely that they had to be abandoned and replaced by new structures. Strong aftershocks continued to rock the region through February 1813.

Relocation of Mission La Purísima

In March 1813, Father Mariano Payeras wrote to Governor José Joaquín Arrillaga and made a strong case for relocating Mission La Purísima to a new location. The new site was in a small canyon, *La Cañada de los Berros* (the canyon of the watercress). It was located across the Santa Ynez River about four miles to the north of the original location. The new site was called Amúu by the Chumash and was noted for beautiful California wildflowers. La Purísima Mission was officially moved to the new location on April 23, 1813. The new site had water resources in the canyon, as well as adequate firewood, lumber, rock, lime and sand for construction purposes. The Los Berros site was not on the edge of a swamp but on sandy, dry ground. There was less fog at this location, and it promised to be a warmer and healthier

In 1813, Mission La Purísima was relocated to Los Berros Canyon, about four miles north of the original location. Structures at this location were massive and well buttressed. The earthquake of 1812 inspired the building improvements. When Edward Deakin painted the mission residence building in the late 1880s, the building was still in good shape, with roof tiles still in place. *Painting by Edward Deakin, courtesy of Santa Bárbara Mission Archive-Library.*

place to live. Los Berros was on the *El Camino Real* road from Santa Inés to San Luis Obispo. Soldiers carrying mail from Mission La Purísima had an easier ford of the Santa Ynez River. Previously, those who forded the river even with knowledge of the terrain had to cross nearly two miles of mire and mud. It often took a whole afternoon to make a river crossing.

RUINS OF MISSION VIEJA

The ruins of the mission founded in 1787 can still be found in the city of Lompoc. Ruins of the original mission quadrangle currently lie between E and G Streets as they intersect with Locust Avenue. A cut made by the construction of the Southern Pacific Railroad exposed more ruins and virtually eliminated the southern end of the original mission quadrangle.

Today, the remains of the church completed in 1803 are bisected by F Street. This street cut through the church ruins in 1960, and an archaeological reconnaissance at the time exposed some of the architecture, including two walls and a tile floor. The 1803 church was originally placed so it jutted into the quadrangle of the mission rather than constituting one wing of it, and a

A view of the ruins of Mission Vieja de La Purísima from about 1880. The view is looking south. Note the quadrangle structure that composed the mission complex. Holes in the walls were for roof timbers. A barn-like structure visible to the right of the photo was added after the mission period. *La Purísima Mission Archives, courtesy of Channel Coast District of California State Parks.*

row of rooms behind the church effectively divided the quadrangle in two. A wall pierced by an arched doorway completed the separation. From early photographs, it appears that the church was two or more stories high. These two-story ruins identified in the early photographs as the 1803 church were probably buildings behind the church. These buildings may have had two stories and possibly even a loft.

Two fragmentary walls are all that is left of the church today. These walls flanking the main entrance show that the façade was made of stone rather than of adobe or brick, and it was covered with lime plaster. A projecting cornice of brick, whitewashed and then painted red, ran across the façade above the arch of the entrance door.

In 1845, the ruins of the original Mission Vieja were renamed *La Purísima Rancho*. Joaquín Carrillo filed a claim for the ranch, claiming land running along the hills above the old mission site and along a road to the new mission site called Camino de la Purísima. This is probably part of what is today State Highway 246. Carrillo's original claim crossed the Santa Ynez River

A view of the ruins of the front of the church from the first La Purísima Mission in Lompoc. The photo dates from the late 1930s. *La Purísima Mission Archives, courtesy of Channel Coast District of California State Parks.*

and included land right up to the mouth of Los Berros Canyon where the current mission is today. In 1849, La Purísima Rancho was finally confirmed to the Carrillos, but it did not include land on the other side of the Santa Ynez River. The rancho consisted of some 4,443 acres and was granted to Joaquín Carrillo and José Antonio Ezquiel Carrillo. Ulysses S. Grant conferred title to the Carrillos in 1873.

Chapter 5

NEOPHYTES AND FRANCISCANS

During 1794–96, a great many Indians became neophyte converts of La Purísima Mission. Frequently, large numbers would be assembled for baptism. In September 1794, Father Lasuén baptized forty adults at La Purísima in one day. Father Fermín Lasuén, as father president of the missions, confirmed neophytes into the Catholic faith only up until 1795. At this time, Confirmation was the formal acceptance of converts into the Catholic faith by a bishop. After 1795, Lasuén could no longer perform this rite. He was only empowered by the church to act in the absence of a bishop to confirm for a term of ten years, and that term expired in 1795. Confirmation was not again conferred at La Purísima until 1844, when the first bishop arrived in California. At this time, twenty-two remaining neophytes were confirmed at the mission.

By 1797, there were one thousand Indians residing at La Purísima. Large numbers of converts came to the mission in 1803–4. Many left their mountain villages to join the mission in 1812 just prior to the great earthquake. The earthquake seemed to draw Indians to La Purísima rather than frighten them away. Missionaries baptized Indians in the ruined church of the mission for nearly four months afterward.

In the twelve years just before the close of the eighteenth century, Franciscan missionaries at La Purísima averaged 108 converts a year. All neophytes over the age of nine were instructed in the rudiments of Christian faith. Women were taught catechism apart from the men. Children had their own hours of instruction. All recited aloud and learned by heart the doctrine of the Catholic faith. Indians sang hymns in Spanish and Latin daily. Neophytes became so used to the moral points of religion, prayers and hymns that they were remembered long after the missionaries were no longer around to teach them.

From 1787 until 1834, when the first Book of Baptisms was filled, only thirty-eight non-Indians, or *gente de razón*, were baptized at the mission, while some 2,345 neophyte Indians received the rite and were recorded in the register. Thirty-three different Franciscan missionaries officiated at the baptisms and signed their names in the register. Not all of these were assigned to the mission. Franciscan missionaries who served at La Purísima were from a variety of places. Many of them were from various regions in Spain: two from Catalonia, six from Cantabria, two from Aragón, two from Burgos, four from Majorca and one from Estremadura. Two friars were from Mexico, and two were from Cuba. Eighteen friars who were assigned to Mission La Purísima are listed below with their dates of service.

FATHER VICENTE FUSTÉR (1788–89) AND FATHER JOSÉ ARROITA (1788–96)

These Franciscan missionaries were the founding missionaries at Mission La Purísima. Neither of them was at the founding of the mission on December 8, 1787. Both of them arrived in 1788 after building commenced at the first mission site. Father Fustér was a native of Zaragosa, Aragón, Spain. Fustér began baptizing neophytes at La Purísima in 1788 and remained there until the summer of 1789. Fray José Arroita, usually known as José, was from the Spanish Franciscan province of Cantabria. His California career consisted chiefly of building the initial Mission La Purísima at its first site, which was destroyed in the earthquake of 1812. Father José served at La Purísima until 1796.

FATHER CRISTÓBAL ORÁMAS (1789–92)

Fray Orámas replaced Father Fustér at La Purísima in 1789. Father Orámas served at La Purísima until 1792.

Father José Antonio Calzada
(1792–96 and 1798–1804)

Fray Calzada was born in Trinidad, Cuba. His first assignment at La Purísima was from 1792 until 1796, replacing Father Cristóbal Orámas. He was posted a second time at La Purísima in 1798 and served until 1804, being replaced by Father Mariano Payeras. Fray Calzada officiated with Fray Arroita over new construction at the first site of Mission La Purísima. From 1794 to 1796, he and Father Arroita constructed a warehouse, a vaulted granary and a room to house equipment for pack animals. The friars added additional rooms for officials, soldiers and missionaries to the mission. They also renovated existing structures and added a brick corridor to the main building.

Father Gregório Fernández (1796–1805)

Father Fernández was a native of Burgos, Spain. In 1796, he was sent to Mission La Purísima after the departure of Fathers Arroita and Calzada. Father Fernández was active in construction at the first site of La Purísima. In 1797, he obtained the services of master weaver Antonio Henriquez. By 1798, mission industries included weaving cotton into cloth and wool into blankets and making shoes.

Father Francisco Uría (1797–98)

A native of Vizcaya, Spain, Father Uría was at Santa Inés when the Chumash revolt broke out at La Purísima in 1824. Hubert Bancroft writes that he "was stout in physique, jolly in manner, addicted to pleasantries and jokes, indulging sometimes in coarse language, kind-hearted and well liked though at times very quick-tempered, and was noted for his generosity, especially to the Indians."

FATHER MARIANO PAYERAS (1804–23)

Father Payeras was a native of Inca, island of Majorca, Spain. After serving at a number of missions, the final period of his life was as a missionary at La Purísima from 1804 until his death in 1823. In 1810, Father Payeras notified his superior, Father President Estévan Tápis, that paganism had practically ceased to exist and there were abundant cattle for food and sheep for wool at Mission La Purísima. After the great earthquake of December 12, 1812, Payeras moved the mission to Los Berros, which is the present location of the restored mission northeast of Lompoc. The official transfer took place on April 29, 1813. At the new site, an entirely new establishment was built. During this period, Payeras composed a catechism in the native Purismeño Chumash language.

In 1815, Payeras became the fourth president of the missions, with thirty-seven missionaries working under him. Much of his time was spent traveling to missions under his jurisdiction. Payeras wanted to extend the mission system into the San Joaquin Valley to serve

A likeness of Mariano Payeras, OFM. Fray Payeras was a native of Inca, Majorca, Spain, founder of the second Mission La Purísima and president and commissary prefect of the missions of California. Father Payeras was originally named Pedro Antonio Payeras Boras. He took the name Mariano after being ordained in the Franciscan Order. The painting is a copy of one that hangs in Inca, Majorca. The original was done about seventy years ago from historical accounts of his likeness. The copy was donated to Mission La Purísima in October 1976 by the mayor of Inca, and it is currently on display at the mission. *Artist Tomás Horrach, photo by author. Permission, courtesy of Channel Coast District of California State Parks.*

an estimated four thousand Indians in that region. In 1819, he approved a request for missions to support presidios and pueblos economically since annual supplies and pay for soldiers was no longer coming to Alta California from Mexico.

During the Bouchard invasion in 1818, Payeras was an active participant in the defense of California. He kept close watch over the insurgents' movements in the Santa Bárbara region and sent forty armed neophytes

to Mission Santa Inés. Governor Pablo Solá praised Payeras's actions and notified the viceroy accordingly. In 1819, Payeras was thanked in the king's name for his services during those trying times. He concerned himself with Russian affairs in the northern part of the territory in 1822. He accompanied commander of the San Francisco Presidio Luis Argüello on a trip to Fort Ross in that year and drew up a long description of the fort and vicinity.

Father Mariano Payeras died on April 28, 1823, and was buried the following day in the sanctuary of the church at La Purísima, which he had reestablished in 1813. At his demise, Payeras was fifty-three years old, having been a Franciscan for thirty-eight years.

Father Boscana was a Franciscan missionary in California. He served at the first Mission La Purísima before the earthquake. Unique as an ethnographer, Father Boscana later wrote a treatise on the origin, customs and traditions of the San Juan Capistrano Indians entitled *Chinigchinich*. *From Robinson's* Life in California.

FATHER GERÓNIMO BOSCANA (1806–11)

A native of Majorca, Spain, Fray Gerónimo Boscana was transferred to Mission La Purísima in 1806 and served until 1811. Boscana is most noted as a Franciscan ethnographer. Those who knew him state that he was an inveterate taker of snuff and was kindhearted, generous and generally well liked.

FATHER ESTÉVAN TÁPIS (1811–12)

Father Tápis was a native of Catalonia, Spain. In 1803, after the death of Lasuén, Tápis became president of the missions, an office he held until 1812. While president, he served at Mission La Purísima and afterward was at La Purísima for about a year. Father Tápis was much loved by religious, military, settlers and Indians. When he could, he taught boys the rudiments of ordinary schooling and wrote music for the singers in the church.

Father Antonio Ripoll (1812–15)

Fray Ripoll was born in Palma, Majorca, Spain. His first assignment in California was at Mission La Purísima. During the Bouchard invasion of 1818, Ripoll trained a company of local Indians at Mission Santa Bárbara to fight the enemy. When Bouchard threatened to attack, Ripoll marched his Indian militia to Santa Inés. Ripoll had a working knowledge of the Chumash language and was well known for his paternal concern for the native Chumash people.

Father Gil y Taboada (1815–17)

A native of Guanajuato, Mexico, Father Gil was noted for having learned the Chumash language well by 1817. While at Mission Santa Cruz before coming to La Purísima, Father Gil occasionally went in disguise into gambling establishments and took a hand in card games for the purpose of detecting the gamblers and confiscating the cards. Being later accused of the charge of gambling, his superiors were inclined to consider him innocent though imprudent.

Father Francisco Román Ulibarri (1818–19)

Father Ulibarri was from the diocese of Calahorra, Spain. He was assigned to Mission Santa Inés from 1815 to 1819 and held a temporary assignment at La Purísima from 1818 to 1819.

Father Antonio Rodríguez (1819–24)

Born at San Luis Potosí in Mexico, Father Rodríguez acted as secretary to Payeras in 1821. Father Rodríguez officiated at the funeral of Father Payeras at La Purísima in April 1823. In 1824, when the Chumash revolt occurred at La Purísima, Father Rodríguez was ill at the mission. Bancroft states, "He was taken by the rebel neophytes and kept for some weeks a prisoner; but was treated with great respect, and worked faithfully for the interests of his flock at the time of their surrender. His kindness of disposition caused him to be well liked by the Indians."

FATHER JOSÉ SÁNCHEZ (1820–21)

Father Sánchez was a native of Old Castile, Spain. At San Diego, he accompanied Payeras on a reconnaissance of the interior country between San Diego and San Gabriel in 1821. Father Sánchez was of cheerful disposition, frank and generous in nature. He was a great sportsman. Socially, he was friendly and fond of a joke, even a practical one.

FATHER BLAS ORDÁZ (1823–24)

A native of the province of Burgos in Spain, Father Ordáz was at La Purísima when the Chumash Indian revolt broke out in 1824. He and his companion, Father Antonio Rodríguez, together with soldiers and their families, took refuge in the mission compound. After a truce with the Indians, he accompanied families to Mission Santa Inés. After Payeras's death in April 1823, Father Ordáz continued work on the residence building at the mission. Bancroft said of Father Ordáz, "Padre Blas was a lively and good-natured man, but his fondness for women involved him occasionally in scandal and reprimand from his superiors."

FATHER MARCOS ANTONIO SALAZAR DE VITORIA (1824–35)

Father Vitoria was a native of the province of Álava, Spain. He was the minister at La Purísima until August 1835. Often in feeble health and not accredited by his superiors with great ability, he was beloved by his neophytes.

FATHER FELIPE ARROYO DE LA CUESTA (1834–36)

A native of the province of Burgos, Spain, Father Arroyo was not only a great missionary but also a distinguished linguist and musician. He had an avid interest in mechanical things. By 1831, Father Arroyo was dividing his time between his religious duties and various ingenious inventions. One invention was a water clock that rang a bell as an alarm at any desired hour. When he was transferred to Mission La Purísima, Father Arroyo had become paralyzed and was in a wheelchair.

FATHER JUAN MORENO (1836–40)

Although born in Montenegro, Old Castile, Spain, Father Moreno became a Franciscan in Mexico. He was one of the last recruits of the California missions from the College of San Fernando. Father Moreno officiated at La Purísima in 1834. He also may have served at La Purísima from 1836 to 1840, but there is no definite record for these years, and the mission had no regular minister. An Indian at Mission Santa Cruz stated that Moreno was very skillful in throwing a *reata* (lasso) and proud of his success in lassoing bears.

Chapter 6

ECONOMICS OF THE MISSION

The crops grown at La Purísima were much the same as those of the other missions of the period. Wheat, barley, corn, beans and peas were the principal agricultural products. Wheat was grown near the arroyos or in canyons where water was available with irrigation. Crude wooden plows tilled the land. Grasshoppers were great pests and decimated planted wheat. Neophytes collected them by hand in large baskets to save the crops. Indian farmers prevented wheat rust from forming in hot weather by reducing moisture that formed on the grain. They did this by running through the fields with stretched *reatas* (leather ropes). This bowed the stalks of grain, which rebounded to shed moisture. The largest harvest record for the mission (13,343 bushels of mostly wheat and corn) occurred in 1813. With approximately forty-six years of statistics compiled, the average crop yield was about 4,100 bushels a year at the mission.

At the old site (Mission Vieja) in Lompoc, there was a fine orchard and vineyard. A vineyard existed at Jalama where olives, pears and walnuts were grown. The mission cultivated almonds, apples and vegetables and herbs such as cabbage, chilies, garlic and mint. Miscellaneous crops included cotton, flax, hemp and indigo.

When Señora Malo de Janssens was interviewed in 1935, she recalled the gardens that existed at La Purísima when she lived there as a little girl from about 1855 to about 1859. Her recollections describe the location of what is now La Purísima Mission State Historic Park. She remembered that nasturtiums, marigolds and French hollyhock, or *malva*

Natives utilize a primitive plow to prepare a field for planting near Mission San Diego de Alcalá. Drawing by A.B. Dodge. *From Zephyrin Englehardt's* San Diego Mission.

real, grew in profusion. She recalled that pepper trees shaded ruins of the mission and gardens.

The mission orchard was noted for its fine pears. The orchard supplied early settlers of the Lompoc Valley. Hogs were fattened on the pears. Brandy was even distilled from pears in *alambiques*, or stills, at the mission.

A mission's material wealth also depended on its livestock. Livestock was classified as *ganado mayor* (major livestock, such as horses, cattle and mules) and *ganado menor* (minor livestock, which included sheep and goats). In this respect, La Purísima did exceptionally well. The mission was famous for its fine stock, especially cattle and sheep. Livestock at the mission were cattle, sheep, goats, hogs, horses and mules. In 1787, the mission began with only 408 head of livestock, which included 166 sheep, 99 goats, 83 head of cattle, 46 horses, 12 mules and 2 hogs. In January 1810, Payeras noted that sheep and cattle numbered 20,000 head, thus providing appropriate clothing and rations for neophytes. In 1819, Father Payeras reported that La Purísima had produced nearly 100,000 pounds (500 *botas)* of tallow. Tallow was sold and used to make soap.

La Purísima often gave surpluses to newly founded missions. La Purísima sent goods to Missions Soledad and Santa Cruz in 1791, and in 1797, the mission sent goods to San Miguel. In 1805, La Purísima sent newly founded Santa Inés Mission numerous products.

With an abundance of wool and a large supply of hides, La Purísima was in an excellent position to manufacture cloth, blankets and leather goods. In 1797, Antonio Enríquez was hired by the mission to teach the art of weaving. Neophytes made blankets from wool and were able to weave cotton cloth of different grades. Indian craftsmen made leather goods and shoes. They made military equipment for the presidios. Indian craftsmen produced boots (or *botas*), saddle pads, knapsacks, leather rain proofs, packsaddles and leather semi-lunar rump covers for horses. They also made saddles and leather tack for horses. For presidios, they fabricated sword scabbards and five-ply white *cueras*, or leather jackets for the *soldados de cuera* of the presidios.

The presidio of Santa Bárbara quickly became indebted to La Purísima. In 1797, the garrison owed the mission more than $400. In 1818, the presidio purchased blankets, shoes, serapes, hides and pack outfits from the mission. Payeras sold saddles, weapons, blankets and mules to soldiers, some of whom resided as far south as the presidio of Loreto in Baja California. The mission also sold corn and beans to the presidios.

Economic systems function only when there is a medium of exchange. Frontiers seldom have sufficient specie to serve the need, and consequently, other media must be used. During the California mission period, tobacco and soap were accepted for this purpose. Money circulating among the troops of the presidio of Santa Bárbara was often in the form of soap and cigars. The same was true of Monterey. A soldier, Augustín Marquéz, in order to pay for a cavalry outfit and weapons that he secured at La Purísima, paid for his purchase in cigars.

La Purísima maintained a store for *gente de razón* (or non-Indians). The names of several prominent Californians of the time appear in the account books. Lieutenant Raimundo Carrillo, Francisco Ortega, Juan Ortega, J.B. Alvarado, Antonio Reyes and others traded there. As indicated, there was little coin in the country, and debts were paid in other media. In 1807, Reyes satisfied his mission creditors with horses or colts at two dollars apiece. All the supplies, of course, were not produced solely at the mission. Each year, ships from San Blas, Mexico—the California base of supplies—brought such things as china, sugar, fine cloth and other commodities, which were exchanged for mission products. In 1810, the Mexican War of Independence began in Mexico. During the decade that followed, the government rarely sent any ships or supplies to California.

Not mentioned in the reports was the illicit trade the mission carried on with foreign ships, especially after 1810. Mission artifacts reveal that English and Cantonese china was common trade merchandise from British and American ships that plied the coast.

Each California mission also derived an income from Indian labor. All that the neophyte produced went to the mission. When Indian labor was hired out to the gente de razón (usually for about twenty cents a day), wages were turned over to the general mission fund. The mission supplied all the neophytes' wants, so the friars believed this practice to be just.

The progress at the mission during the years from 1817 to 1819 was made when Father Payeras was the lone resident friar at La Purísima. Occasionally, the industrious friar made trips to other missions, but he would always hurry back to his beloved La Purísima. Neophytes at the mission needed his constant attention. While serving them, he never neglected the industrial and commercial affairs of the establishment.

TRADE AND OUTSIDE INFLUENCES

The Spanish began to promote the collection of California sea otter pelts at about the same time that La Purísima was founded. Sea otter fur was highly prized throughout the Orient. A plan was hatched calling for California Indians and others to hunt sea otter while missions and presidios stored the furs. Officials were to gather pelts for shipment to the Orient and exchange them for quicksilver to be used in Mexican mines. Franciscans in California objected to the plan when they found that it resulted in serious exploitation of the Indians both in and out of the missions. The plan eventually failed, but the Indians continued to be harassed by even more aggressive hunting and trade tactics of "foreign" merchants who appeared along the coast in increasing numbers after 1795.

Spanish edicts prohibited foreign involvement in the lucrative sea otter trade, but the edicts were ignored or circumvented by French, Portuguese, English and American traders. Black market activities flourished, and the accompanying violence and corruption further undermined the situation of those Indians who lived along the coast. Channel Islanders were especially affected because the islands were unprotected by Spanish military forces and were, therefore, a perfect base of operations for both hunters and traders.

By 1810, Russian and American interests dominated the trade, and Aleutian Islanders were imported to hunt sea otter on a year-round basis. Unlike the Chumash, the Aleuts went about the business of hunting sea

Mission Indians unloading cattle hides for the hide and tallow trade. *Artist Jo Mora, unknown date.*

otter on a large-scale, highly organized basis. They brought their spears and their hide-covered, oceangoing *bidarkas*, or canoes, along with them on the Russian and American ships. As a result, the remaining Channel Island Chumash found their lives so disrupted that they were forced to abandon the islands and make new lives for themselves on the mainland. Many of them cast their lot with the other Chumash Indians at La Purísima, Santa Bárbara and Santa Inés Missions.

Irregularities in ship supply from New Spain after 1810 also forced the mission to seek trade with outsiders. Over time, La Purísima developed a clandestine trade in hides and tallow to secure from foreigners the commodities it could no longer obtain from Spanish-approved sources. Indians herded and slaughtered cattle, tanned hides and boiled down the fat of carcasses for candle tallow. In exchange for these products, missionaries received iron and metal, tobacco, rope, clothing and other goods. Through the hide and tallow trade, the products of mission Indian labor entered the international economy.

Chapter 7

RANCHES, LANDS AND ROADS OF LA PURÍSIMA

The first mission of La Purísima at Algascupi was situated at a site off the El Camino Real (or the King's Highway) to the south of the Santa Ynez River. Father Mariano Payeras described Algascupi as an open canyon without protection from northeast to southeast, allowing wind and fog from *Punta de Pedernales* to envelop the immediate hills. Located on the edge of a marsh, Mission Vieja was exposed to cold winds, more in summer than in winter, and fogs made for oppressive winters.

In 1802, Mission Vieja boasted a garden roughly two hundred yards square surrounded by an adobe wall. Water for it was obtained from Miguelito Canyon, which was adjacent to the mission. In 1808, Payeras reported that he had irrigated the rancho at Salsipuedes and that it would soon be productive. About the same time, he accepted administration of the Reyes rancho near what is now Casmalia. Here he obtained mares for breeding, horses for work and cattle to be slaughtered for hides and tallow. In 1809, the rancho supplied about 1,000 *fenegas*, or 1,500 bushels, of corn. The best resources were located on the opposite side of the Santa Ynez River from Mission Vieja. Payeras mentioned that a farm, five minor livestock (or sheep) ranches, most of his livestock and almost all of his crops were located across the river from Mission Vieja.

By 1810, Father Payeras had transplanted the vineyard from Algascupi to a place called San Francisco (Jalama). The vines did well at the new location, and he made a life contract with the Ortegas to take care of them and produce wine and brandy for the mission. Payeras, in a letter to Father

President Estévan Tápis in January 1810, indicated that the wine was being made in new presses using a Majorcan method of winemaking. The Jalama vineyard was located about eight miles south of what is currently La Purísima Mission State Historic Park. In 1854, it was mentioned in a survey as being roughly seventeen acres in size. Adjoining Jalama two miles west was a second mission vineyard. It was listed in the survey of 1854 as the San Franciscita vineyard at a size of about five acres.

By 1814, La Purísima counted 4,652 head of horses, the greatest number of horses ever reported in any one year for any of the missions. Two years later, 9,000 head of large stock were at the mission, and sheep numbered 11,000 head. La Purísima sheep herds would eventually grow to roughly 12,000 head. Sheep were tended from five temporary sheep camps located north of the Santa Ynez River. Fernando Librado, a Chumash Indian interviewed by the ethnologist John Harrington, indicated that the mission used the mouth of Honda Canyon as a horse pasture. Alfred Robinson, in his *Life in California*, observed in 1834–35 that Guadalupe was a cattle ranch of Mission La Purísima.

MISSION CAMPS, PASTURES AND RANCHES

In 1818, ranchos of the mission extended fourteen leagues (approximately thirty-six miles) from north to south and six leagues (fifteen and a half miles) from east to west. The Mission Account Book lists a granary at Los Alamos as early as 1824. Wheat and lima beans were grown there. When the mission estate was valued in 1834, the following ranchos were listed: Sitio de Misión Vieja, Sitio de Jalama, Los Alamos, San Antonio, Santa Lucia, San Pablo, Todos Santos and Guadalupe.

La Purísima eventually grew to hold dominion over between 200,000 and 300,000 acres, which included eleven ranchos varying in size from 4,500 acres to 50,000 acres. There were two vineyards and an anchorage at Cojo Bay that also supported the mission. The jurisdiction of the mission covered lands west of Gaviota to Point Conception, east toward the Highway 101 alignments and north to the Santa Maria River.

During the years of operation, Mission La Purísima raised wheat, barley, corn, peas, garbanzo and fava beans. Winter wheat became the most valuable crop, followed by corn and barley. Mission agricultural sites naturally gravitated to watercourses such as San Antonio Creek. Rancho San Antonio initially served as a farming outpost for the mission. It was located in what became the Rancho Todos Santos. Mission use of this locality may date from 1802. In 1810, Father Payeras noted that a granary and outbuildings for farmhands were built at the site. The mission sent a group of neophytes to live at the farm and raise grain crops. The Chumash had to leave the farm every two weeks to attend church services at the mission.

In 1802, Juan Francisco Reyes received a rancho, which became part of La Purísima Mission holdings when Father Payeras purchased the land from him in 1808 for 2,000 pesos. In a letter dated January 13, 1810, Payeras wrote of the Rancho Reyes to the father president of the missions, Estévan Tápis. According to Payeras, the rancho had a good source of water for irrigation, allowing for good crop growth of corn, wheat and barley. Father Payeras renovated the old ranch building and roofed it with tiles. He also raised livestock at Rancho Reyes, which included horses for work and mares for breeding. The rancho allowed for the augmentation of cattle herds. Cattle were slaughtered at the rancho. Hides were traded and tanned to provide leather for the manufacture of leather goods.

Rancho Reyes was part of what later became Rancho Casmalia and was located in Shuman Canyon. In October 1809, according to the La Purísima Mission Account Book, Antonio Reyes (whose father sold the Reyes tract to the mission) received goods from the mission. This transaction closed the Reyes account at the mission and thereby gave La Purísima complete possession of the *La Larga* tract, which implies that the Reyes family originally controlled La Larga before the mission acquired it. La Larga is near what is now Guadalupe. Payeras first mentioned the La Larga tract in January 1810 in a letter to Father Estévan Tápis when he commented on a large water ditch against the sandbanks of *Oso Flaco*.

In 1813, Payeras noted that the new site of La Purísima at Los Berros was closer to the Rancho San Antonio, which produced much grain and was also closer to the pastures of La Larga. In April 1813, according to the Mission Account Book, the mission contracted to have five hundred head of cattle delivered to La Larga. In 1817, Rancho de Larga was nine leagues (or about twenty-three miles) from the mission at Los Berros. It was near the Camino Real and provided a way station for the comfort of travelers. In 1817, a hostel was constructed there for travelers of palisades and tules.

Early Trails and Roads

The Santa Ynez River mouth was a major obstacle to travelers during mission times. Travelers had to wait for the tide to become low enough to cross the sandbar where the mouth of the river met the ocean. In this period, trails to reach the new ranches and farm outposts were limited to canyon corridors and watercourses such as the San Antonio Valley and primarily ran along an east–west axis. New roads unfolded slowly due, in part, to the rugged nature of the natural terrain. Sergeant Pablo Antonio Cota performed surveys in 1788. He established the part of El Camino Real that connected Mission La Purísima with Missions Santa Bárbara and San Luis Obispo. In this same year, Cota established a seasonal road from Lompoc and the Santa Ynez Valley into Santa Bárbara over the San Marcos Pass. Fray Estévan Tápis and Felipe de Goicoechea, comandante of the Presidio Santa Bárbara, later used the trail in 1798 to perform a survey of the Santa Ynez Valley in order to choose the new site for proposed Santa Inés Mission. Mission Santa Bárbara had a vineyard and an *asistencia* on the Rancho San Marcos in the Santa Ynez Valley. The San Marcos route was used regularly to travel to the asistencia.

In 1804, a new version of El Camino Real opened over the mountains at Refugio. The road connected the New Mission of Santa Inés to Mission San Luis Obispo. It followed a route on the opposite side of the Santa Ynez River from where the first mission at La Purísima had been established. Prior to 1804, the Camino Real followed the original Portolá route along the coast. By 1810, commercial interests at La Purísima extended the old Camino Real route from the first mission site through Salsipuedes Canyon west to the ocean and the vineyards of Jalama and San Franciscita and to the ship anchorage at Cojo. After establishing the second mission at La Purísima in Los Berros Canyon in 1813, travel between the central coast missions was much easier. It was still necessary, however, to ford the Santa Ynez River to access the ship anchorage at Cojo and vineyards near Jalama.

Local residents also used a secondary trail system. Travelers used La Purísima Canyon and passed through the La Purísima Hills to Graciosa and Harris Canyons, avoiding the San Antonio area. Another road ran from the original mission location, past the new Berros Canyon mission site to Rancho San Antonio by way of Santa Lucia Canyon and then branched north to Shuman Canyon near what is now Casmalia. This road led to the grain and cattle ranches in the San Antonio Valley, Casmalia and Guadalupe districts.

Two mission-period trails are of historical note in the La Purísima area. In the north, a trail ran along San Antonio Creek west to the ocean. From this point, the trail hugged the coastline and then turned northeast near Mount Lospe. In the south near the Burton Mesa area, a second footpath may have run between Rancho San Antonio south past Huerta Mateo to Mission La Purísima at Los Berros and the Santa Ynez River. Spanish settlers and explorers probably adopted an Indian trail network of Purísmeño Chumash villages, such as Kesmalia, Lospe, Saxpil and Lououato. This trail would have continued south along today's Highway 1 corridor through what became Rancho San Julian and then turned west, where the route headed to the ocean at Jalama.

Chapter 8

INDIAN LIFE AT THE MISSION

M ission La Purísima was founded under the administration of Father President Fermín Lasuén, who replaced Junípero Serra after his death. Serra taught Indian neophytes at the missions by having them watch and imitate the actions of the Spanish as they cleared fields, sowed and harvested grain, carted produce and made adobe bricks. Serra relied on soldier-appointed *mayordomos* who lived at the missions to teach more specialized tasks such as tanning and shoemaking. Lasuén, on the other hand, brought artisans from Mexico to teach trades and skills. Thus, La Purísima received the benefit of contract carpenters, masons and weavers. Artisans imparted crafts and skills to local Indians, who, in turn, taught other Indians. The neophytes at La Purísima were patient and careful craftsmen and willingly worked at jobs assigned to them by the mission padres.

The multiple Indian languages spoken at La Purísima challenged the priests to learn Indian tongues, and the padres employed interpreters to communicate with neophytes. The Chumash were impressed by the strange mysticism of the Franciscans and willingly took part in the mission's religious ceremonies. At La Purísima, Indian musicians and church choirs were a continuing source of pleasure to the padres. The senior priest usually devoted time to cultivating a choir. Indian men were chosen by the priest for their ability to replicate European sound in song and received instruction in Spanish as part of choir training. Eventually, the neophytes of La Purísima were taught to play European instruments, such as flutes, violins and various percussion instruments for rhythm.

Neophytes were given considerable freedom during the first years at La Purísima. In all but the harvest season, they were allowed as much time off as they desired. They were permitted to collect seeds and prepare native food items that had been part of their customary diet. Those who remained independent of the mission, however, found it difficult to live in the old way due to continuing spread of Spanish settlement. Mission holdings extended over vast areas. Rancheros took up the best native sites. Cattle grazed the hills and valleys, trampled waterholes and devoured favorite seeds and seed-producing plants of the Chumash. Native discontent erupted in September 1794 when twenty neophytes of La Purísima and San Luis Obispo, together with a band of gentiles, were arrested for inciting revolt at San Luis Obispo. Five of the agitators were sentenced to hard labor at the local presidio.

ROUTINE LIFE OF PURÍSIMA INDIAN NEOPHYTES, CIRCA 1800

In 1800, Father Hora of Mission San Miguel accused the Franciscan missionaries of mistreating Indians. Charges reached the viceroy, who directed Governor Diego de Borica to investigate. The governor complied by requesting commanders of the four presidios to answer fifteen questions on the subject. Comandante Felipe de Goicoechea of Santa Bárbara reported that the La Purísima fathers were guilty of mistreating the Indians. Friars there were requested to explain their version of the controversy. After studying both reports of the army and the missionaries, the viceroy felt that the charges were unfounded and exonerated the Franciscans. The controversy produced a valuable snapshot of the routine life of the neophyte Indians at Mission La Purísima up to the year 1800, when the report was completed.

Father Gregorio Fernández of La Purísima, who himself was accused of being overzealous with Indian converts, filed a report in which he said that Franciscan friars taught Christian doctrine to neophytes in their own languages. Padres attempted to teach neophytes Spanish. Neophytes, however, conversed in their own languages and in a jargon that was a mixture of Mexican, Otomite, Lipan, Apache, Comanche and several other languages that were commonly used among the troops.

Indians were only given a limited time to roam outside the mission. Mission Indians were fed daily *atole* and *pozole*. Atole was a mixture of water and dried grains and was served for the morning and evening meals. Pozole was a porridge or thick soup of wheat, corn and beans or horse beans and meat. Pozole was typically served for the midday meal. In addition, extra wheat rations were given on Sundays and feast days. La Purísima neophytes were also allowed to collect wild seeds in season.

For clothing, the neophytes were given a woolen blanket and suit of cotton cloth, which, when treated with care, lasted more than a year. In addition, the men were given two breechcloths of Puebla woolen cloth or of cloth from the mission. The women and girls received gowns and skirts and a blanket like the men.

Habitations of the Indians were of tule reeds and much the same as they had been when the Indians were living in their pre-colonial villages. Adobe buildings were constructed to store crops, provide workshops and store various goods. The apartment for the single women (*monjerio*) was a room fourteen yards square. The interior walls were lined with bunks constructed of boards where mats were spread to allow for a comfortable sleeping situation. Personal necessities were also stored in the habitation. After prayers, single men retired to their homes or to the community kitchen (*pozolera*). Often, they remained to sleep in the corridors, which, like the pozolera, was outside the cloister or inner courtyard of the mission.

La Purísima's neophytes worked four or five hours a day. Work hours were less for pregnant, nursing or aged women and children. Mission Indians were permitted all kinds of popular diversions. Almost half the year was granted to them for gathering wild seeds in various seasons outside the mission complex.

La Purísima Indians were permitted to negotiate with Spanish soldiers and settlers and were taught how to deal with them. They were given permission to approach the guards. Soldiers were allowed services of the neophytes for chores when they asked. There were times, however, when Indians were over-burdened with work by the soldiers. During these times, neophytes were able to challenge the tasks and to stop work if it was excessive.

Neophytes were punished if they left the mission furtively. The padres observed that such excursions, especially at night, produced bad results. Indian men often would forsake their wives, solicit and lead away women or steal and do other things opposed to good order.

Punishments applied included whipping, shackles and being locked up. Punishments were given for theft, running away and concubinage. The corporal of the guard at the mission was notified for transgressions against the common good, which included the killing of cattle or sheep and the burning of pastures.

By 1804, the mission settlement at La Purísima included 1,520 Indian converts. In that same year, Padre Mariano Payeras arrived. He was a man of unusual zeal, vision and practical ability. Under his leadership, the mission entered a period of unprecedented material prosperity. Franciscans already grew wheat, corn, peas, beans, grapes, pears, peaches, olives and fruit at other California missions. La Purísima, however, had an unreliable water supply, which hampered agricultural activity. Payeras immediately improved the irrigation system and dramatically increased the quantity and quality of food available for neophytes. Mission La Purísima gained prestige when Father Mariano Payeras was appointed father president and later *comisario prefecto* of the missions of California.

Father Payeras was able to maintain excellent relations with La Purísima's neighbors, notably the Ortegas, who had established their rancho near the little harbor of Refugio in 1797. Payeras opened up opportunities for local trade and other forms of mutual assistance. Livestock prospered at the mission and increased as never before. Mission industries prospered as well. Soap, candles, wool and leather products became leading commodities. Weaving became a major industry at the mission. Indians worked on rather crude Spanish-style looms. Over the years, some forty thousand wool blankets were manufactured at La Purísima, along with cotton material for clothing.

POPULATION AND DIVISION OF LABOR OF INDIANS AT THE MISSION

In 1804, 1,520 neophyte Indians were residing at Mission La Purísima. Smallpox, measles and other health problems soon took a heavy toll. From 1804 to 1807, there were about five hundred neophyte deaths recorded. This amounted to about one death for every three Indians living at the mission. Overcome by fear and disillusionment, about 200 mission Indians left La Purísima and returned to the hills. Payeras did convince many of the runaways to return to the mission. Nevertheless, the neophyte population began to decline. By 1812, the Indian population at La Purísima was down to 999. When the mission moved to its new site at Los Berros across the Santa Ynez River in 1813, 1,010 neophytes resided at the mission. By 1818, only 937 neophytes were there. The population continued to decline so that by 1824, only 662 neophytes remained at the mission. In 1842, La Purísima still had about 60 neophytes left.

Neophytes at La Purísima held a number of different jobs as they participated in the mission community. *Alcaldes* (Indian leaders) were elected to govern other Indians within the mission. From 1813 to 1816, three different alcaldes were noted in the baptismal records. Priests required the services of an *ynterprete* (interpreter) when preaching to other Indians. During Mass, Indians served as singers (*cantores*). For special ceremonies, neophytes were witnesses for weddings (*testigos*) and godfathers (*padrinos*) or godmothers (*madrinas*) for baptisms. A male nurse (*enfermero*) tended the sick at the mission. A house servant (*paje*) saw to the needs of the mission padres. *Sacristans* managed the sacristy of the church and took care of vestments and church-related items needed for the saying of Mass. Indians were cowboys (*vaqueros*), bread makers (*panaderos*), blacksmiths (*herreros*), carpenters (*carpinteros*) and cooks (*cocineros*) for the padres. Some Indians were poultry raisers. They had their own chickens and supplied the mission with them when they were needed.

Alfred Robinson, the author of *Life in California*, observed Indian vaqueros at the cattle ranch of "La Purísima called Guadaloupe" in 1834–35. He found them busy at their annual cattle slaughter (*matanza*). Indian vaqueros were mounted on what Robinson described as splendid, well-trained horses. When the foreman (mayordomo) pointed out an animal for slaughter, a

Indian vaqueros, or cowboys, at Mission La Purísima. *Drawing by Jo Mora, unknown date.*

vaquero with dexterous precision would lasso it by the horns while another entangled the feet to drop the animal. Escaping animals were lassoed on the run and pulled down by reining in the horse suddenly. More expert vaqueros could drop an animal by grabbing a steer's tail and spurring the horse to upset it.

By 1813, some mission neophytes were living in adobe apartments with two rooms at the new mission site across the Santa Ynez River. These apartments were arranged in a line of two long housing structures, with each structure containing about ten apartments. Some twenty family housing units existed in these two structures. The southernmost housing structure was probably built first and had an extension of some rather large rooms that were most likely an infirmary. The infirmary was listed in the 1816 annual report of the mission. Nothing identifies which neophyte families lived in the twenty adobe housing units. In 1816, there were about 257 neophyte couples at the mission. Only 8 percent of these families could reside in the housing. Most likely, neophyte families with some degree of status were chosen to occupy the residences.

FORMATION OF INDIAN MILITIA AT LA PURÍSIMA

In 1816, the commander of the presidio at Santa Bárbara, José de la Guerra y Noriega, reported to Governor Vicente de Solá a list of people in the district who were capable of bearing arms against a potential pirate invasion of the coast. Only 1 soldier was listed at La Purísima with two pistols, a musket and a sword. There were, however, 109 others at the mission who carried eight pistols, twenty muskets, four lances and twenty-one swords. This was most likely the Indian militia. La Purísima Mission was perhaps the best-armed location in the entire presidial district at that time.

In 1818, La Purísima provided forty-one armed neophytes to Mission Santa Inés in anticipation of a raid at the Ortega Rancho by the Argentine insurgent Hippolyte de Bouchard. During the period of the invasion by Bouchard, La Purísima Mission resources were at the disposal of the government. This included provisions, pack animals and horses. Neophytes went into an encampment in the mountains and joined Sergeant Carlos Carrillo to contain the enemy, which did attack the Ortega Rancho at Refugio. Neophyte militiamen were armed as lancers and archers. They maintained a watch along the coast and

Mule pack trains were an effective way to transport goods and supplies at Mission La Purísima. Muleteers (*arrieros*) managed the pack trains and were skilled at using the animals for transport. *Etching by Ed Borein, courtesy of the Santa Bárbara Mission Archive-Library.*

helped evacuate those who were in danger of being raided. The militia also made mail deliveries.

In 1822, there were six soldiers stationed at La Purísima as the escolta or soldier guard. Father Payeras felt that this garrison would hardly afford adequate protection in case of a great emergency. He thus came up with a rather elaborate scheme for strengthening the military defenses at the mission by formalizing a plan for an Indian militia. The Payeras plan called four *partidas*, or divisions, to this militia. The first partida was to consist of thirty natives from the Santa Bárbara Presidio. Eighteen of these were to be armed with bows and arrows, and twelve were mounted with lances and reatas. The second partida was to consist of fifteen to thirty vaqueros or others who were good horsemen. They were to be armed with lances and provided with strong reatas and should go by the name of *partida de lanceros de la Purísima*. The third partida was to be a band of fifty natives under forty years of age, familiar with the Spanish language, armed with bows and arrows and called *flecheros volantes de la Purísima*. The fourth and last division, *partida de reserva de flecheros*, was to be made up of the remaining available persons, especially those familiar with firearms. This last division would assist the officials (alcaldes and *regidores*) of the mission, escort persons leaving the mission and act as reserves as needed.

Chapter 9

INDIAN REVOLT AT THE CHANNEL MISSIONS

The Mexican Revolution in 1822 trumpeted the "Plan of Iguala" to indigenous Indians. The Iguala plan called for Indians of Mexico to be considered "new citizens." Following the death of Father Payeras in April 1823, lack of movement of neophytes toward becoming "new citizens" frustrated the hopes of the neophytes at La Purísima. Those frustrations may have been a motivating factor in the Chumash revolt of 1824, when the mission was taken over by neophyte revolutionaries for nearly a month.

Separate letters from Fathers Blas Ordáz of Mission Santa Inés and Narciso Durán of Mission San José identify Prokhor Egorov, a Russian deserter from Fort Ross, as an instigator of local Indians. Father Payeras noted that Egorov was one of the Russians coming through La Purísima. Egorov even worked at Mission Santa Bárbara before joining Indians in the 1824 uprising. Like other Russians who visited California about that time, Egorov may have held with the popular ideas of freedom and equality that were circulating in his homeland. His views may have added to the desires of mission Indians to gain greater liberty as "new citizens" in the Santa Bárbara area.

Indians of the Santa Bárbara area revolted in 1824. The revolt was the most widespread against local authority in the history of the California missions. Ultimately, three missions were involved: Santa Inés, La Purísima and Santa Bárbara. From the statements of old Californians, it was obvious that the movement was a concerted attempt on the part of the Indians to wipe out the power and presence of the Hispanic population and to return to their former pre-colonial liberty. Governor Argüello confirmed that the purpose of the revolt was for the Indians to rid themselves of domination by the gente de razón. Missionaries attributed the real cause of the revolt to be the discontent of the Indians because of demands made upon them to support the military. Supplies for the garrisons from Mexico ceased after 1810. The Indians bitterly complained that they had to work so that the soldiers might eat and that nothing was paid them for their toil and labor, whereas formerly they had been compensated.

Franciscan missionaries protested but gradually realized that they were helpless to obtain any effective remedy; some were so discouraged that they contemplated retiring from California. Mission Indians sensed the helplessness of their plight and, for the first time in forty-five years of Hispanic occupation, planned a revolt to overthrow that dominance. A trusted Indian servant warned José de la Guerra, commandant of the presidio of Santa Bárbara, of the pending revolt, but he ignored the warning.

The revolt began at Santa Inés Mission on February 21, 1824, following the flogging of a Purísima neophyte by order of Corporal Velentín Cota. A native account of the revolt from the ethnographic notes of John P. Harrington implies that a duplicitous Indian sacristan at Mission Santa Inés may have also fueled the revolt. He was said to have informed local Indians that they were all going to be punished by the priest, and then he informed the priest that the natives were going to shoot him with arrows.

In his *Memoir of Mexican California*, Antonio María Osio gave an account of the 1824 revolt. According to Osio, Father Francisco Xavier Uría was just settling down for a 2:00 p.m. nap at Mission Santa Inés on February 21, 1824, when an Indian servant startled the friar with the news that local Indians were in revolt and were about to kill him. Father Uría jumped from his bed and looked out his window and was shocked to see a throng of Indians, painted and equipped with arrows, heading toward the door of his house. Father Uría was a religious man, but he made a habit of using vulgar words so that the Indians would not take advantage of his kindness. As a practical man, Father Uría owned his own musket, which he immediately pressed into service.

At the critical moment, he armed a layperson with another musket and shot and killed the first Indian who set foot on his threshold. The effective force of this musket blast caused the attackers to hold back a bit. Uría did not waste any time. He readied a second shot, aimed and fired his musket at one of the better-painted Indians who had shot an arrow at him. The Indian was killed instantly. The layperson was hit with three arrows and

Right: Raphael Solares demonstrates the use of a bow for ethnographer Léon de Cessac in 1877. Indians such as these spearheaded the revolt at Santa Inés in 1824. *Courtesy Musée de l'Homme, Paris.*

Below: During the revolt of 1824, Mission Santa Inés was set on fire by revolting Indians. *Painting by Russell Antonio Ruiz, 1974, courtesy of his son, Russell Clay Ruiz.*

began bleeding from his mouth. Father Uría pulled two of the arrows out of the man's chest and draped some pieces of deerskin around his neck, which served to keep him from being killed by additional arrows that struck him.

Meanwhile, Father Uría's musket shots were becoming more accurate and deadly. He was quickly loading and firing his musket, his arms moving even more skillfully than they did when he was collecting alms. Fortunately, the Indians retreated, and so he went out into the hall. Father Uría noticed that one of the Indians armed with a musket was stalking him. Uría scurried behind a pillar and was able to fire at and hit the Indian stalker. The soldiers living on the mission grounds were also active. They were well protected from arrows, which did not penetrate their *cueras* (a type of jacket fashioned from six or seven layers of leather sewn together). When the Indians realized that they did not have an advantage over the barricaded father, layperson and soldiers, they decided to set fire to the mission. They set various parts of the homes ablaze in an attempt to give them an advantage. Just as the flames were reaching their greatest intensity, Sergeant Don Anastasio Carrillo arrived with a squad of soldiers. He had been sent to reinforce the Santa Inés garrison in anticipation of the outbreak of the revolt. Since the rebels were not expecting him, they fled. Later, those who had not taken part in the uprising appeared and asked for some tools to put out the fire. They managed to do so but only after two-thirds of the main buildings had been destroyed.

Revolt Spreads to Mission La Purísima

Indians at Mission La Purísima found out very quickly that their neighbors at Santa Inés Mission had revolted. They began to paint themselves and prepare for war at their mission. La Purísima Indians were very fond of the two fathers at the mission—Father Blas Ordáz and Father Antonio Rodríguez—and Corporal Tiburcio Tapia of the mission guard (escolta) because of the corporal's great honesty and generosity. They promised the corporal that, if he turned over his weapons, he would be treated with as much respect as the Indians intended to show the fathers. The Indians held in contempt the four other soldiers of the escolta and their families, as well as the other gente de razón at the mission. Revolting Indians argued that it would be impossible for five men surrounded by a throng of angry warriors to defend themselves. They warned Corporal Tapia to surrender or be killed with the rest of the soldiers. Corporal Tapia was undaunted by the large number of warriors and their angry threats. He was not about to surrender his weapons and told the warriors that his soldiers would never surrender out of fear. He replied to the Indians that he was prepared to resist and that they could begin to attack whenever they wanted.

The battle began with five determined men courageously resisting attack. The Indian warriors could not dislodge the five combatants in spite of their greater numbers. Instead, Indians set fire to soldiers' houses, expecting them to rush over to protect their families. Intense flames quickly consumed timbers in the houses, and tile roofs of the houses collapsed. As the last house that was sheltering soldiers and their families began to burn, Corporal Tapia instructed the defenders to abandon it for the ruins of the first homes that had been burned. Double-checking the exit, the soldiers fired a lively round, forcing the Indians to take cover. Women and children covered with blankets and leather from chairs ran through a shower of arrows and were so frightened that they did not feel burns on their feet from the embers of the burning building. Only one woman was injured. While covering her child with some of her blankets, she was struck by an arrow, which penetrated her belly. The wound was not serious, and she quickly recovered.

Unable to dislodge the soldiers from their positions, the warring Indians tried another attack. When that failed, one of the chiefs petitioned Corporal Tapia for terms. This came at an opportune time since the soldiers had run out of ammunition. The Indians offered to let everyone go unharmed for the safety of Mission Santa Inés if soldiers would hand over their arms. Corporal Tapia again replied that he "preferred to die rather than earn the reprimand of his superiors."

Next, the warring Indians appealed to the young Father Ordáz. They asked him to talk to Corporal Tapia, and if he agreed to terms, the warriors would not go back on their word. Father Ordáz consented to try to negotiate. He convinced the soldiers to hand over their arms with the condition that the priest would not leave their side and would accompany all the besieged to Mission Santa Inés. With these understandings, everyone went to the father's house and handed over their weapons.

When the Indians had all the weapons in their possession, they refused to comply with their promises. They rushed the door of Padre Blas Ordáz's house, but he was able to close it in time to stave off the attack. As Padre Ordáz turned around, he found himself surrounded by the women of the besieged kneeling and begging for confession of their sins. Acting in good faith, the padre consented to the request. All the confessors, terrified and confused, began to speak out loud at once as if each was alone with the father. The poor souls, imprudent because of fear, began disclosing compromising secrets. Some of the confessions of the women disclosed things that their husbands who were present should not know. The father quickly ordered all to be quiet and simply recite an act of contrition instead of confessing so that he could grant them absolution.

Next, the father turned his attention to the attacking Indians. Calling to the leader, in whom he had confidence, the father spoke kindly to him. The friar was aware that the leader was an alcalde and had some standing at the mission, and he opened the door to converse with the renegade band of Indians. The father spoke in a superior manner and reprimanded the Indians for compromising their word and good faith. The alcalde addressed himself to the opposing Indians and took them to task for the last decision they had made. After the alcalde conferred with the hostile band of Indians for a while, he turned and said, "Father, I have just assured them that you will fulfill your word. Now leave quickly with your people for Santa Inés. I will accompany you until you are almost there. Let's go then, before the Indians change their minds again." The father knew his neophytes very well and did not want to waste a favorable opportunity, so he set out immediately with his group. They walked, despite the fact that some of the women in the party had no skin left on the soles of their feet. They walked briskly in that condition until they arrived safely at their destination.

The day of the revolt, the hostile Indians killed two *hombres de razón* who worked at La Purísima. They also killed a member of the Sepúlveda family of Los Angeles, who, unfortunately, was returning from Monterey on foot. This incident was regarded as a major crime. Determined to defend themselves and not be subjected to punishment, the hostile Indians barricaded themselves with whatever they could find nearby.

The fathers had purchased two cannons. They always had enough gunpowder to fire one as a celebratory salute to the patron saint and on other solemn occasions. A native artisan named Pacomio mounted these cannons on very fine carriages and then placed them in a redoubt constructed by an Indian stonemason named Mariano. The redoubt was constructed as perfectly as if an engineer had done it. Those who had been able to obtain firearms formed a company of marksmen. They formed their parapet with the roof planks of the main house, creating embrasures as necessary and always keeping themselves protected by the tiles of the roof. They believed themselves to be as safe there, offensively and defensively, as if they were in a great fort.

Revolt Spreads to Mission Santa Bárbara

Indians from Santa Bárbara began their attack on the very day and hour upon which they had previously agreed. They were aware that everyone already knew of their intent and planned to do battle against them. The presidio was very close, only a gunshot away, so the soldiers posted at the mission were easily joined by those from the garrison. The families of the soldiers remained in place at Mission Santa Bárbara without experiencing the scare suffered by the families at Santa Inés and La Purísima.

A Carrillo brother-in-law of Captain José de la Guerra y Noriega gave the following account of the Indian revolt in Santa Bárbara. He noted that when the captain left the presidio to fight the Indians of the mission, the battle began with little zeal on either side. There was simply a leisurely exchange of long-range gunfire, without any consequence or bloodshed. After a few minutes, the noon bell tolled, and a voice called out, "Cease fire!" After the captain's order had been obeyed, he took off his hat and began to recite the "Angelus." Apparently the meal hour had arrived, and they had to fulfill that obligation first so that they might return to firing later with more vehemence. In fact, they returned to fight "English style"—that is

When the Indian revolt of 1824 spread to Mission Santa Bárbara, Captain José de la Guerra y Noriega from the presidio in Santa Bárbara directed the attack on the Indians at the mission. At the toll of the noon bell, soldiers retired for lunch and then began the attack again after lunch and forced Indians to flee the mission. *Drawing by Alexander Harmer, unknown date.*

to say, with full stomachs. The method must have been very effective because the soldiers fired with much more energy than they had been before eating, and the Indians fled.

Most of the fugitives did not stop until they reached the *tules* in the San Joaquin Valley. Others, who considered themselves very brave, went to the general barracks of Mission La Purísima. They enthusiastically waited there for the impending attack against the mission.

Governor Sends Troops from Monterey to End the Revolt at La Purísima

Reports sent to the governor informed him of everything that had happened at the rebellious missions. Governor Argüello ordered cavalry and infantry companies from Monterey to La Purísima, sending with them artillerymen to handle a cannon. Lieutenant Don Mariano Estrada commanded all the troops. Proceeding to Mission La Purísima, he took up a position on the most dominant point, a gunshot away from the mission homes.

Englehardt, in *Mission La Concepción Purísima*, described the military actions at the mission during the revolt, as compiled by Lieutenant Estrada. Lieutenant Mariano Estrada assembled his troops at Mission San Luis Obispo. There were 109 artillery, infantry and cavalry troops with a four-pounder field piece. The expedition left Mission San Luis Obispo on March 14, 1824, passing the night at Oso Flaco. Here they intercepted two hostile Indian couriers who were coming from San Luis Obispo. On March 15, the march continued and set up camp at the foot of Cuesta de la Graciosa.

Early in the morning of March 16, Lieutenant Estrada managed to drag the cannon by hand over the "declivity of the mountain" and place it undercover for protection along with munitions. A corporal and twenty-eight horsemen were left guarding the cannon. Lieutenant Estrada commanded two advance guards that separated into a pincher movement to attack La Purísima Mission. Step by step, they approached the mission until they were within firing range of the cannon. At this point, the cannon was moved into position, and they began firing at about 8:00 a.m. Gradually, artillery was moved forward until some thirty-three infantrymen were within musket range of Mission La Purísima. From their loopholes, Indian hostiles poured out lively gunfire at Lieutenant Estrada's positions. Hostile Indians fired a one-pound cannon and also sent out a shower of arrows. Estrada replied with his artillery and the good aim of his musketry.

Soon the Indians wanted to take flight but were completely cut off from doing so. Father Antonio Rodríguez, the missionary at Mission La Purísima, was approached by the hostile Indians to seek terms, and a written request for cease-fire was sent to the attacking force of Spanish soldiers. At about half past ten o'clock in the morning, Father Rodríguez appeared in person and managed to stop the attack.

The casualties of the battle against 400 (Englehardt estimates only about 150) Indians were 1 dead and 2 wounded. On the side of the rebels, 16 were killed and a considerable number wounded. Two *pedreros* (swivel guns) were taken, besides sixteen muskets, 150 lances, six machetes (cutlasses) and an incalculable number of bows and arrows.

In his *Memoir of Mexican California*, Antonio María Osio adds another perspective to Estrada's account. La Purísima Mission was situated between

A Spanish four-pound field cannon (*cañón de campaña*) at Mission San Gabriel in Los Angeles. This type of cannon could fire both solid and canister antipersonnel rounds. Solid shot was effective at several hundred yards and was successfully used against revolting Indians at Mission La Purísima in 1824. *Courtesy of Rachel Titiriga. Modified from original.*

two low ridges in a narrow ravine. Indian rebels constructed their redoubt there, and it was impossible for them to defend themselves from cannon fire aimed at them from the ridges. They realized the problem as soon as the soldiers fired the first shots, so the Indians quickly abandoned their position and sought refuge at the main house (presumably what is now the residence building). Here Indian marksmen, who stationed themselves on the top floor, tormented the troops the most.

Lieutenant Estrada, out of consideration for the venerable Father Rodríguez, whose bed was directly below the feet of the Indian marksmen, did not allow Flores, his best artilleryman, to dislodge Indians with the cannon. The father was too old and sick to be able to get up from his bed. However, when Estrada saw one of his soldiers die from a shot that passed clear through his chest to his back, he decided that he must order the cannon fired. A cannon shot hit about halfway up the slope of the roof, directly above where the Indians were firing. Because of the way the homes were constructed, a huge portion of the main wall was blown apart. The severity of the blow caused the building to shake and the Indians to tremble. Thoroughly frightened, the Indians did not know what recourse to take. Their preferred maneuver was to flee, but this was impractical for them because they were completely surrounded. Two more cannon shots were directed at the pillars of the corridor in an attempt not to destroy the building or have any of the debris fall on Father Rodríguez. With this, all the Indians lost their nerve, with the exception of one whose conduct deserves mention.

Entering the church, the Indian fixed his gaze on a Christ figure about a foot in length. Addressing the figure, the Indian sought its protection by hanging it covered around his neck, promising to faithfully serve the church if he should survive an attack on the Spanish soldiers. Approaching within arrow range of the soldiers, the opposing Indian continued fighting alone until he had shot the last arrow in his quiver. Then he immediately turned around and walked at a normal pace toward the church. Many shots were fired at him, but not one found its mark. The Indian later fulfilled his promise to the church by serving as a loyal sacristan and living an exemplary life as a true Catholic until he died.

Other Indians were panicked by the power of the cannonballs and did not know what to do. Finally, they begged Father Rodríguez to go and intercede for them, but when he showed them that he could not even stand up, they decided to carry him out in his own bed. In this manner, the Indians brought him to Captain Don José de la Guerra y Noriega, who had just arrived and taken command. After listening and agreeing to a number of Father Rodríguez's requests, Captain de la Guerra assembled all the now disarmed Indians in an attempt to discover the identities of the principal instigators of the revolt. When de la Guerra found out who they were, he ordered them shot on the spot. Others were exiled in perpetuity to various presidios, where they were sentenced to a period of forced labor. The rebel Indians, Pacomio and Mariano, were assigned to the Monterey Presidio, where, on account of their good behavior, they found steady employment.

Governor Argüello was sent a communiqué detailing everything that had occurred. He had the pleasure of learning that the rebellious Indians at the missions had been brought under control. The fugitives, however, in the tules were yet to be caught. There was no alternative but to go after them. The company from the Santa Bárbara Presidio was ordered to join the operation. Captain de la Guerra was put in charge, accompanied by a chaplain. The departure took place as soon as the necessary provisions had been prepared. When the expedition arrived at the tules, the commander decided to use gentle measures to attract the Indians. Renegade Indians did not want to return to the missions and expressed the low regard in which they held the inhabitants of California. They did, however, hold the Reverend Father Vicente Sarría in high regard for his many virtues. Only he had the necessary power of persuasion to calm the Indians' fears. The commander made several promises, assuring them of their safety and promising to forget the events of the past. The rebellious Indians were persuaded to return to the missions, and everything ended peacefully. Several promotions resulted for military personnel involved in the revolt of 1824. As a result of the insurrection, neophyte weapons were removed from the missions to presidios by orders of the governor as a precautionary measure.

It was Osio's opinion in his *Memoir of Mexican California* that the Indians of Alta California, especially the adults, who were called Christians simply because they had been sprinkled with baptismal water, were never true Catholics. Osio maintained that the Indians left their rancherías and errant lifestyles for the missions out of fear, deceit or self-interest. Neophytes listened to the fathers preaching the gospel, but they did not understand what was being said. The words were foreign to many Indians, and they were translated poorly. Often, neophytes really did not believe in the meaning of the words that they did understand, especially those regarding faith. In Osio's opinion, the strongest conviction of the Indian was "what was visible was real." Osio also states that catechists of the Catholic faith never gained the attention or earned the reputation of better-known *hechiceros* (witch doctors). According to Osio, Indians eagerly sought out the hechiceros to hear them describe favors that the devil bestowed on those who served him well.

A Chumash Leader of the Revolt Becomes a Model Mexican Citizen

José Pacomio Pogui actually led the Chumash revolt of 1824. He was an extraordinary man. He first distinguished himself as a boy at La Purísima, and the Franciscans taught him to read and write. At age eighteen, missionaries apprenticed him to a Spanish carpenter, and within four years, he had mastered the craft of carpentry. He was a great favorite of the clergy and the military at the mission, and he received training in carpentry from the missionaries and in musketry from the soldiers.

When he chafed at Franciscan rule, Pacomio helped put together the most inclusive anti-colonial rebellion in the history of the region, involving hundreds of Indians at several missions. According to Vallejo in his *Historical and Personal Memoirs,* José Pacomio Pogui was one of the indigenous leaders at Mission La Purísima. He was credited by some later accounts with being the main planner and instigator of the entire revolt. He was patriotic in his ideas and felt that he was destined to free his country. He pursued his rebellion and took advantage of his new rights with uncommon skill and vigor.

In the early 1820s, he sent emissaries to all the indigenous peoples living in the vicinity to organize the revolt. He is supposed to have told Father Rodríguez, who stayed at La Purísima during the revolt, "Better a hundred casks of blood should flow than it should be a hundred thousand. If in this war I kill all the whites, not over four thousand persons will perish, but if the whites win and kill off all the Indians, many hundreds of thousands of human beings with souls made in the likeness of God, as I have been told by the missionary fathers who educated me, will lose their lives."

For his crimes at La Purísima, Pacomio was banished from Santa Bárbara to serve time at the presidio in Monterey. He was sentenced to ten years hard labor at the presidio and exile. A decade after the revolt at La Purísima, José Pacomio was again a carpenter, living in Monterey with his wife and seven other Indians, at least three of whom were from the Santa Bárbara region. José Pacomio also owned livestock, for he registered his own cattle brand with the municipality of Monterey. In 1833, he was one of the members of the town who called for an expedition against horse thieves preying on the region's ranchos. He became a member of the *ayuntamiento* at Monterey. In 1836, he won appointment by the Monterey town council as a *comisario de policía*, and in 1833, 1839 and possibly the intervening years, he voted in municipal elections. Of his public service, General Mariano Vallejo recalled that he acted with "judgment and perspicacity." José Pacomio's skill as a tradesman, his Spanish literacy and his ties to Mexican officials help explain the arc of his life as he moved from outlaw resistance leader to accepted Mexican citizen.

Chapter 10

SECULARIZATION OF
MISSION LA PURÍSIMA

B y the mid-1820s, the majority of the Indian population along the
central coast had either been born at the missions or had spent the
past two decades as part of mission communities. The Chumash subgroups
with the least acculturation to the mission system were Indians from the
Channel Islands, who mostly arrived at the missions between 1814 and
1816. Extensive mission agricultural activities resulted in the creation
of small settlements and work camps where Indians lived to tend fields,
orchards and livestock that were located at distances too great for daily
commute to the missions. The Chumash subgroups

Mission life had trained the Chumash population in agricultural
subsistence practices, Spanish language and dress and Catholic religious
observances. Having achieved some facility in Spanish cultural ways, there
arose increasing restlessness on the part of the neophyte Indians for political
and economic independence from the missions. The unsuccessful Chumash
uprising in 1824 led to a realization among the Indian population that they
could no longer return to their former way of life.

The administration of José María Echéandia, governor of California
between 1825 and 1830, brought the beginnings of emancipation for the
mission Indians. The missionaries opposed his secularization efforts. They
maintained that although acculturation had to proceed, the Indians still
were unprepared for citizenship in California's Mexican society. They also
well understood that the Hispanic settlers' desires for mission lands were a
major motivation for the secularization movement.

Echéandia's first efforts were to set at liberty a few Indians who appeared to be most able to provide for themselves and serve as full Mexican citizens. These Indians came to be known as *licenciados*. At least two of these, one from La Purísima and one from San Buenaventura, gained their freedom by marrying daughters of non-Indian residents. A third, José Pacomio Pogui, a carpenter from Mission La Purísima and a banished leader of the 1824 Chumash uprising, settled in Monterey after serving his sentence at the presidio there.

Although there were some moves toward secularization on the part of Governor José María Echéandia beginning in 1825, it was not until his successor became governor that secularization of the California missions actually occurred. Full secularization of the missions did not occur until the administration of José Figueroa, who served as governor of California between 1832 and 1835. The temporal affairs of the missions were removed from missionary control and placed in the hands of commissioners appointed by the governor. Indian neophytes were not automatically freed but could become licenciados based on the recommendations of the commissioners and missionaries according to their ability to support themselves. Indian pueblos or *barrios* (neighborhoods) were established with lots for houses and gardens provided to each family. Annually, an alcalde, two regidores and a collector were selected for economic government within these Indian communities. Freed Indians were still obligated to assist in sowing and harvesting mission crops and in providing personal service for the missionaries. Each family was to receive its own fields for sowing crops, and pastureland for community livestock was also to be provided.

Little documentation exists regarding the actual implementation of Figueroa's emancipation regulations in the Santa Bárbara District. Missions Santa Bárbara and La Purísima were secularized in 1834. La Cieneguita (near Hope Ranch in Santa Bárbara) became the Indian barrio for the Barbareño neophytes, while the largest portion of Purisimeños gathered at Los Alamos. Smaller groups of Barbareños and Purisimeños remained in rancherías adjacent to the missions.

A letter dated November 30, 1834, referred to the ex-mission of La Purísima as the "Pueblo de la Purísima." Domingo Carrillo was listed as *comisionado*, and Father Marcos Antonio Vitoria was listed as *ministro*. By 1835, the term "Pueblo de los Berros" was being used for the Purismeño Indian community. In 1834–35, Alfred Robinson visited Mission La Purísima and made the following observation in his book, *Life in California*:

In the morning we rode over to the Purísima, where we found two reverend friars, Fathers Vitoria and Juan Moreno. This mission was originally established in 1787, at a place now known as "La Mision Vieja"; but has since been rebuilt in its present location, and though possessing abundant wealth, in cattle and planting grounds, yet has been much neglected, and the Indians generally are ill clothed, and seem in the most abject condition. We remained here but a short time, and returning to Santa Ynez, slept there that night, and the next day reached the ship.

Subsequently, La Purísima Mission lands were parceled out to various Mexican rancheros, although a small amount of land was given to some of the Indians. These changes led prominent Spanish families to seek opportunities for landownership. Joaquín Carrillo and José Antonio Ezquiel Carrillo had been trying to secure the abandoned Mission Viejo land for years. In 1873, Ulysses S. Grant finally conferred title to 4.443 acres of this land known as the La Purísima Rancho to the Carrillos.

In 1839, only 242 Indians still reported as living at Mission La Purísima. In 1844, the Purismeño Indian community, both at the ex–Mission La Purísima and at its Rancho Los Alamos, was decimated by a smallpox epidemic, causing an estimated 75 percent reduction of the Indian community. Smallpox attacked California Indian populations in the north for three consecutive years from 1837 to 1839. The disease was introduced in the Russian colonies north of San Francisco. It also entered Monterey in 1844, presumably from a ship. The epidemic killed many, especially Indians, and subsequently spread as far south as the Purismeño district. Smallpox vaccination was known at the time, and those who were vaccinated were able to survive the epidemic, but nevertheless, many neophytes perished. Most of the surviving Purismeños dispersed to work as servants and ranch hands for the gente de razón.

In October 1845, Governor Pío Pico issued his *Reglamento* for final dismantling of the mission communities. Pico's Reglamento provided unconditional release for all the mission Indians, leaving them free to remain in communities associated with the missions or to establish themselves wherever they chose. They were to be treated like other citizens and paid for their labor. Many worked as vaqueros, laborers and domestic servants for the non-Indian population, and a few plied their trades learned at the missions. By 1852, when the California state census was taken, only 12 farmers were noted among the 168 Indian men for whom occupations were listed. Most listed themselves as vaqueros, servants or laborers. Other professions mentioned were carpenters, masons, shoemakers, saddlers, cooks, bakers, shepherds, fishermen, a blacksmith and a violinist.

On November 2, 1845, two ex-neophytes, Pastor Shoy'ama and his son-in-law Elceario, petitioned for a grant of land eight hundred varas square (about 111 acres) at the site of the former mission of La Purísima to include an orchard and vineyard that they had tended for many years. The petitioners had survived the devastating smallpox epidemic, and it is likely that they inhabited the neophyte family housing at the mission. They were among the last of the mission Indians to reside at La Purísima. Pastor and Elceario sold their land grant in 1848.

Pastor Choyama (Shoy'ama) was born at the village of Guaslaique in Foxen Canyon and baptized at Mission La Purísima in 1790 at the age of ten. He died in 1858 and was buried at Mission Santa Inés. Pastor was listed only twice as a padrino, and according to Fernando Librado (a famous Chumash informant who knew him in his later years), Pastor had been a judge or alcalde at La Purísima. This was not recorded in the mission records.

Fernando Librado told linguist-ethnographer John P. Harrington several stories about Pastor Choyama. Pastor's Indian name was Shoy'ama, which meant "jackrabbit nose." Pastor opposed the custom of Chumash shamen (*alchuklash*), who were particularly important in the naming of children, curing illnesses and other Indian mysteries. The alchuklash were all from Santa Cruz Island. An alchuklash went about to various villages to see how people were getting on. He would see if anyone was sick and so forth. Soon after the birth of a baby, the alchuklash was summoned while all the relatives were still present. As soon as the child was born and laid out, the alchuklash knew by watching it under which planet it was born, and as soon as the child moved, he gave it its name. When an alchuklash named a child, he gave advice to the parents so that when the child reached adulthood, it would be well advised and be a good person. The alchuklash was usually an old man and judged the destiny of the child. This was done without ceremony or speech, as far as Fernando knew.

After La Purísima was secularized, Pastor lived for a time in a cabin not far from the mission. Once, when Fernando was working for Ramón Malo at Rancho Purísima as a cook, Pastor came to visit him in an abandoned part of the mission. He came every morning to Fernando's kitchen to get some fire. One morning, he came bringing with him a tile. Fernando gave him a good jolt of whiskey, and then Pastor began to ask him questions about his grandfather, his name and so on. Pastor liked cigars, and he spoke broken

Spanish. He often repeated his words many times in a low voice. Pastor died in Santa Bárbara, an old man who could hardly walk.

Librado told Harrington of the fatherly advice Pastor provided him on several occasions and that when Pastor died, it was he who buried him. It is likely that Pastor was still at Mission La Purísima into the later half of the 1850s, well after he and Elceario had sold their land grant.

Under the last Mexican governor of California, Pío Pico, the majority of La Purísima was granted to Ramón Malo and Juan Temple in 1845. Juan Temple of Los Angeles originally purchased it for $1,100. José Ramón Malo purchased land from Juan Temple and moved to La Purísima with his family. Malo was one of the first settlers at the mission. Originally from Ecuador, he came to California from Mexico after hearing of a "land rush" that would follow in the wake of secularization of the California missions.

In 1935, the daughter of Ramón Malo was interviewed, and her statements concerning early ranch life at La Purísima were published in the *Los Angeles Times*. Señora Josefa Malo de Janssens was eighty years old when interviewed, but her memory was vivid concerning her life at La Purísima.

Señora Janssens was born at La Purísima on May 31, 1855. She was the youngest of eight children in her family. She remembered Indians still at the mission when she was a child. "Oddly enough," she stated, "all the women were named Maria! There was the cook, Maria Theodora, and the faithful sewing women, Maria Antonia and Maria Kuku." Señora Janssens further commented that when she was seven, a lame Indian taught her to smoke cigars (*cigaros*). "The boys were not the only ones who 'hid out' for that pastime!" she commented.

On every eighth of December, the date of the founding of La Purísima, a gala festival would be held at the mission. Señora Janssens recalled that the Indian musicians—Baltazar, Venansio, Cecilio and Luis el Cantor (probably mission Indians)—would get out the old mission violin, viola, drum and triangle to accompany the singers. Also two pipe organs with bellows, which were turned by a crank, were used on such occasions.

One of the Indians specifically mentioned by Señora Janssens was Fernando Librado. Fernando was known as one of the last of the Purísima Indians. Señora Janssens dispelled the comment that Fernando was 111 years old when he died. She stated that he was perhaps a little more than 80 at his death.

A tintype of Fernando Librado was donated to La Purísima Mission in 1962. The tintype had the comment "110 years old" written on it. Information with the tintype photo of Fernando Librado stated that as a

Fernando Librado was one of the last of the Purísima Indians. He led a colorful life and provided several accounts of early days at the mission. *Tintype image, La Purísima Mission Archives, courtesy of Channel Coast District of California State Parks.*

small boy, he was rescued from the Channel Islands and educated. At one time, he was said to have gone to Washington, D.C., as a representative of the Chumash Indians. During the fiestas that were held in December at the mission, Fernando was one of the singers. On one occasion, the sister of Señora Janssens, María de Jesús Cota, met Fernando in Ventura. Fernando lived in Ventura just before his death. She observed that he had a huge dictionary under his arm and that he had paid twenty pesos for it. "*¿Para qué quieres ese libro, Fernando?*" (What do you want that book for, Fernando?) asked María Cota. "*Para saber cosas, señorita*" (To know things, miss), was the dignified reply.

Señora Janssens recalled rodeos at La Purísima when the Picos, Cotas, Carrillos, de la Guerras, Danas, Ybarras and Ruizes all came and had much fun. After Ramón Malo died in 1859, his family left La Purísima. The mission became almost abandoned, and the remaining Indians moved to Santa Inés and to a reservation at a place called "Zanja de Cota," which is now the Chumash Indian Reservation in Santa Inés.

After the takeover of California by the United States in 1846, the rights to the former mission lands were once again in dispute. The Catholic bishop of California, Joseph Alemany, made claims on the property of many of the former missions. In the case of La Purísima, he was eventually awarded several specific portions of the former mission, including the old priests' quarters and adjoining buildings, the former church and adjacent cemetery, the vineyard and the old warehouse but not the land in between. After two decades of legal haggling, the Catholic Church was formally granted its claim on January 24, 1874. The property was subsequently sold nine years later to Eduardo de la Cuesta in 1883. Sometime after that, the Union Oil Company acquired the property, which was later deeded over to the State of California.

Chapter 11

LA PURÍSIMA MISSION GARDEN

The National Park Service spearheaded restoration of Mission La Purísima in 1934. Under the auspices of the National Park Service, restoration was accurate in almost every detail. Design of the mission garden, however, deviated from that concept. Historical evidence suggested that the original mission surroundings were rather bare and dusty due to the scarcity of water and Indian population that inhabited the area. For purely historical reasons, a bare and sparsely planted area surrounding the restored buildings was considered the best treatment. This, however, would be of little interest to visitors of the mission. It was, therefore, decided to construct a sample garden that was representative of all the California missions. Included in the garden plots were native California trees, herbs and shrubs. During the year 1938, some twenty thousand visitors traveled to the park and showed as much interest in the garden as in the restored buildings. The typical mission garden was clearly a success.

Ed Rowe, senior foreman and landscape architect, was given the task of creating this garden. He obtained reproductive stock from original plants growing at or near the missions and at some of the old ranchos. Artichokes, for example, came from near Mission Santa Inés. The Castilian rose was from Mission San Antonio. Kapolini cherry was from the Ortega Rancho at Arroyo Hondo. Fig trees were reproduced from a tree found growing at Mission Santa Clara. Grapes came from Jalama Canyon, where the remains of an old wine vat are still to be found today. White oleander was from a shrub that grew in the garden of Pió Pico, the last Mexican governor of

California. Olive trees were from stock that grew at Mission Santa Bárbara. Pomegranates came from Mission San Antonio and the Juan Dana home. Seedling oranges were duplicated from the Indian orchard near the old San Marcos Pass, which were the oranges planted in Spanish times.

At La Purísima, there is a lone surviving pear tree of an orchard that grew just north of the mission buildings. It is still visible today. Ed Rowe took cuttings from original trees at Missions San Juan Capistrano, San Juan Bautista, Santa Inés, San Luis Obispo and Carmel. He grafted these on seeding pear stock. Consequently, many of the pear trees currently in the mission gardens are pear varieties form other missions. Mission Vieja de la Purísima (site of the original La Purísima Mission) was studied as well for leads on early plantings of the mission. Old Indians asserted that there were no creeks for irrigation anywhere in this part of the country, except from mountain springs. Water for the first mission was originally obtained from what is now Miguelito Canyon and Salsipuedes Canyon, which was fed from the Santa Ynez River. There is some speculation that water tables may have shifted after the great 1812 earthquake. A local informant remembered that farming only took place near the arroyos and in the bottomlands. An entry in Thompson and West's 1883 *History of Santa Barbara and Ventura Counties, California* relates the following:

> *The zealous Catholic missionaries did a great deal of work in building, irrigating, and planting out trees. They had a magnificent orchard and alameda, or avenue, where Truitt's land begins at the mouth of the* cañón. *Its disappearance is thus accounted for: After Mexico gained her independence as a republic, the church grants reverted, the missions were sacked and unroofed, and the land were placed in the hands of commissioners, one of whom, Carrillo, took such a fancy to Lompoc that he retained it. Fearing that the presence and maintenance of the fine orchard might give the church authorities* prima facie *claim to the land, it was ruthlessly cut down. There was also a fine vineyard about where Mr. F.S. Balaam now lives, which was destroyed by fire. Quite recently (1883) some of the vines were to be seen. The Jalama between Lompoc and Point Concepcion light-house, has still a neglected vineyard and olive, pear, and walnut orchard. The Bishop claimed it until T.B. Dibblee traded other property for it.*

The mission garden concept established at La Purísima is now over seventy years old. It clearly set a precedent for historic gardening. In 2003, a similar project began at Old Mission Santa Bárbara. The Huerta Project established a garden that focused on heritage plants of the missions. My book *Changes in Landscape: The Beginnings of Horticulture in the California Missions* helped define the project. The Huerta Project used a similar model to that established at Mission La Purísima. Subsequent mission garden projects were developed in California, at El Presidio State Historic Park in Santa Bárbara, and at the Mission Garden Project in Tucson, Arizona.

Inspecting La Purísima restoration in 1934 from right to left are Ed Rowe, H.V. Smith, Ed Borein and Leo Carrillo. Ed Rowe developed the mission garden. H.V. Smith was project superintendent for the National Park Service. Ed Borein, noted cowboy artist, watches Leo Carrillo, local descendant and film personality, ring the bell on the restored residence building. *From La Purísima Mission Archives, courtesy of Channel Coast District of California State Parks.*

Chapter 12

RESTORATION OF
MISSION LA PURÍSIMA

The mission buildings began to fall into ruin after 1836. By 1904, roof tiles had been removed from the residence building. Subsequent rains eroded away the structure so that by 1934, it had become a series of shapeless mounds of brown adobe overgrown with weeds and brush.

MISSION RECONSTRUCTION
AND THE CITIZENS ADVISORY COMMITTEE

Realizing the historical importance of La Purísima Mission, Union Oil Company deeded the property to the County of Santa Bárbara with the understanding that the county would secure federal aid for a restoration project. The county subsequently deeded the land to the State of California, and additional acreage was purchased. The State Park Commission asked seven prominent Santa Bárbara residents to form an advisory committee for the proposed park in September 1935. The La Purísima Citizens Advisory Committee released a report outlining a proposed restoration policy and advocating the complete reconstruction of the site, as opposed to simply excavating and stabilizing the remaining ruins. The National Park Service and the State of California used the report as the basis for the master plan to develop the mission ruins. The La Purísima Mission Citizens Advisory Committee continued in operation for nearly sixty years, advising on restoration and land acquisition. Major members of the committee in the early days included Pearl Chase, local civic leader; Mark Harrington, curator of the Southwest Museum in Los Angeles; and Edith Webb, famed author of *Indian Life at the Old Missions.*

In the early 1970s, I was an interpretive specialist at Mission La Purísima. For three consecutive years, I operated seasonally with grants from the La Purísima Mission Citizens Advisory Committee to organize collections and establish an archive at the mission. I produced a final report in 1973 entitled "La Purísima Mission State Historic Park Archives: An Experiment in Interpretation and Preservation." The archive is still operative at La Purísima, and the collections are open for research by appointment. I served on the La Purísima Mission Citizens Advisory Committee and was its secretary for many years.

Dr. Mark R. Harrington, noted archaeologist and curator of the Southwest Museum in Los Angeles, was an early member of the La Purísima Citizens Advisory Committee. He worked in conjunction with the National Park Service in the early 1930s to supervise archaeology at the mission prior to restoration. *From La Purísima Mission Archives, courtesy of Channel Coast District of California State Parks.*

LA PURÍSIMA MISSION BECOMES A CCC PROJECT

The Civilian Conservation Corps (CCC) and the National Park Service began rescuing the crumbling remains of the mission complex in November 1934. The National Park Service assigned a staff of historians, archaeologists, engineers and architects to dig out the facts of the mission's original structure. After nearly a year of study, they developed the plans from which CCC Company 1951 rebuilt the entire mission. CCC enrollees used original tools and methods whenever possible. When the restoration was completed, the mission was turned over to the State of California to be administered as a historic park. More completely restored than any other mission, La Purísima is, in fact, the largest and most complete restoration in the West.

CCC HISTORY AT LA PURÍSIMA

By 1938, the Los Angeles District had some twenty-three CCC Camps. Nine of the twenty-three were National Forest Service camps. Five were Soil Conservation camps. Six were Park Service camps. Two were National Monument camps. One was supervised by the Department of Grazing.

The camps associated with La Purísima were Companies 2950, which was a Soil Conservation camp, and 1951, which was under the jurisdiction of the Park Service. The unique project of the Los Angeles District was considered to be the restoration of La Purísima Concepción by Company 1951 at Camp Purísima, SP29. Company 2950 was formed in April 1936 and was transported from Fort MacArthur to Camp Lompoc (site of the current La Purísima Mission). For the first several months, the camp fought forest fires. Company 2950 merged with Company 1951 in May 1937. After the merger, the La Purísima CCC company (camp) became known as the "Twin Camps."

With up to two hundred men involved in the massive job of reconstruction and restoration, the work went on for several years. The first major project, the residence building, was complete in 1936; the water system, fountains and cistern in 1938; the church in 1939; shops and quarters building in 1940; and the monument residences and other miscellaneous jobs, including the interior decoration of the church, in 1941. CCC enrollees made 110,000 adobe bricks, 31,000 roof tiles and 15,000 floor tiles by hand for the residence building alone.

Late in 1941, on the eve of the 154th anniversary of its original founding, La Purísima Mission was ceremoniously opened to the public as a state historic monument. After the outdoor festivities, religious services were given in the restored church for the first time in 105 years. The date was December 7, 1941—the day the Japanese attacked Pearl Harbor and the United States entered World War II.

Work continued on mission restoration with additional building and reconstruction into the 1990s. All the major buildings were rebuilt and furnished as they were in 1820. Livestock of the period roam the grounds. The original water system was restored, and over nine hundred surrounding acres were acquired as a buffer zone. La Purísima became a State Historic Park in 1963. Today, with a very active living history and crafts demonstration program, mission docents play host to nearly fifteen thousand schoolchildren who visit the mission every year.

An isometric diagram of the original mission residence building showing materials and methods of construction of the original structure. *U.S. Department of Interior, National Park Service, June 1938.*

GLOSSARY

aguardiente: From the Latin *aqua ardens*, or "fiery water." During the mission and rancho period of California history, the term was used for distilled spirits made from the wine of the mission grape. This was the hard liquor most commonly available to Americans here during the gold rush period. The Spanish term may refer to any form of distilled spirits. It is used in this publication to refer to brandy as produced by the missions. Alfred Robinson in his *Life in California* calls it "a powerful California brew."

alambique: A still used at La Purísima Mission to create brandy from pears.

alcalde: An elected Indian authority within the mission having governing authority over other Indians. Alcaldes possessed a real, if limited, authority in supervising the mission Indians and in maintaining order.

alférez: The lowest rank of a commissioned officer in the Spanish army, equivalent in rank to an ensign or second lieutenant.

almud: A unit of dry measure representing about 4.2 quarts. It was one-twelfth of a fanega.

alpechín: The mixture of oil and water after pressing olives for oil.

apostolado: A set of paintings of the apostles.

arroyo: A brook, rivulet or small stream.

asistencia: Also known as a *visita* or a mission substation. Asistencias were associated with larger mission parishes and were designed to serve those in remote areas.

atole: A cooked mixture of water and ground, dried grains; a staple mission food given to neophytes at La Purísima for morning and evening meals.

ayuntamiento: A town council.

barranca: A deep ravine or canyon.

barrio: As used here, a small Indian village after secularization of the missions. It is also synonymous with the term pueblo.

bodega: A cellar, wine cellar or wine vault.

bota: A leather container consisting of a single cowhide used for storing or shipping tallow. The contents weighed about two hundred pounds.

cabo: Corporal.

calinche: A drink made from the fruit, or *tuna*, of the prickly pear cactus.

Canaliño: A name used by European explorers and settlers to identify Chumash peoples who lived in the Santa Bárbara Channel area. The word is also used today by some researchers to refer to the group of Native Americans who lived in the Channel area thousands of years ago and who are probably ancestors of the Chumash.

cañón: A canyon.

cantor: A singer in church services who was often a neophyte Indian.

Chumash: This name originally was applied to the native inhabitants of the Northern Channel Islands only. The mainland Indians used several other names (e.g., Lulapin for the Ventureño and perhaps others; Shmuwush for "coast Indian" for the Barbareño; and Samala for the Inezeño). John Wesley Powell originally used the name Chumash, and Alfred Kroeber continued in this usage. Kroeber's *Handbook of California Indians*, published in 1925, established use of "Chumash" as broadly to refer to all the people speaking Chumash-related languages.

cocinero: A cook, probably for the priest, since this was normally not a male occupation within the Indian population.

colgadura: A cloth wall hanging used in a church for decoration.

comisario prefecto: A commissary prefect; after 1812, the superior prelate of the Franciscan order in California who dealt with the provincial government.

comisionado: A deputy or commissioner. As normally used in California, he was a noncommissioned officer serving on detached duty as a magistrate of a pueblo or villa.

compadre: The term by which the godfather and godmother address the father of their godson or goddaughter and by which the father and mother address the godfather. Also means "protector," "benefactor" or, popularly, "very close friend."

cornucopia: A lighting fixture of mirrors with a candle sconce attached.

crucifix: A representation of Christ on the cross.

cuartel: Barracks or garrison.

cuera: A leather jacket fashioned from between five to seven layers of deerskin to protect the soldado de cuera who served at presidios and missions on the California frontier.

diseño: A description and sketch that was used to identify a claim for land.

don/doña: A title of respect. In California, it was accorded to any Spaniard, officer or person from an important, respected family. Used before the first name. Can also be used to express extreme respect or extreme disdain.

enfermero: An Indian male nurse who tended the numerous sick at the mission.

escolta: The military guard assigned from a nearby presidio for mission or pueblo protection. It consisted of a corporal and from five to seven soldiers.

fanéga: Approximately 1.575 bushels. For Spanish measurement, it is also 12 almunde.

flecheros volantes de La Purísima: A division (*partida*) of militia at Mission La Purísima, literally meaning flying archers of La Purísima.

ganado mayor: Major livestock, which include horses, cattle, donkeys, burros and mules.

ganado menor: Minor livestock, which included sheep, swine and goats.

gente de razón: Literally, reasonable people; in California usage, it meant non-Indian or civilized.

grano: A monetary unit of silver. One peso was ninety-six granos. One real was twelve grano.

hechicero: A wizard or sorcerer; the pejorative name given to Native American shamans by the missionaries.

informe: A general term that refers to the annual report of the state of a mission district.

jacal: A hut or crude dwelling often made of brush and hides.

lagar: A wine, olive or apple press.

league (legua): A Spanish normal league is equivalent to 2.59699 miles or about 5,000 varas. It was considered by Spanish explorers to be 5,000 steps. Traveling by horseback, a league was approximately equivalent to the distance traveled for one hour over level terrain at a normal gait. Some sources indicate that there was also a long league of approximately 4 miles in length.

licenciado: As used here, an Indian who has obtained his freedom from the mission system. A few Indians were given this distinction when Echéandia was governor of California just prior to secularization of the California missions.

lienzo: A painted wall hanging of canvas that was hung in front of the church as a backdrop for *nichos* (carved niches for statues).

madrina: Godmother.

mayordomo: A custodian of civic property, also a foreman of a hacienda or mission.

memorias: List of items to be ordered or supplied; a want list.

Michumash: The word from which the term Chumash originated. It refers to those people who lived on Santa Cruz Island.

milpa: A plot of land, grain field or cornfield.

Mission Vieja: Literally means "Old Mission." This is the term used for the first site of Mission La Purísima Concepcíon, which was destroyed by the earthquake of 1812.

molino: A gristmill.

neophyte: A term used for mission Native Americans who were new followers of the Christian religion.

nicho: A carved niche that framed a statue in a church.

padrino: Godfather.

padrón: A mission register of neophyte families that was like a census.

page or paje: An Indian house-servant for the mission fathers.

panadero: A baker or bread-maker.

paqwot: A Chumash term referring to the leader of several villages.

partida: A division of Indian militia at Mission La Purísima.

partida de lanceros de La Purísima: A division of Indian militia at La Purísima who were vaqueros armed with lances and reatas.

partida de reserva de flecheros: A reserve division of Indian militia a La Purísima who were familiar with firearms.

pedrero: A light gun up to about a three-pounder, normally mounted as a swivel gun but can also be mounted on a field carriage. Literally meaning stone thrower, this term can also refer to a large-caliber bronze mortar.

peso: A monetary unit of silver equivalent to ninety-six granos or eight reales, hence the term "pieces of eight reales." In the first half of the nineteenth century, a peso was equivalent to one U.S. dollar and two Russian rubles.

pozole: A porridge or thick soup of wheat, corn, beans or horse beans and meat. This bill of fare was the normal midday meal for neophytes at mission La Purísima.

Purisimeño: The name applied to mission Indians from La Purísima.

ranchería: An Indian settlement where dwellings are not permanent and are scattered some distance from each other.

rancho: A settlement or a ranch. During mission times, ranches could be used for livestock or for agriculture and typically included vast holdings of land. Often, several ranchos were attached to the various missions. Some of them were privately held during the Spanish period in California. Many more were granted to individuals during the Mexican period in California.

Rancho del Rey: A rancho operated by the local presidio for the support of the soldiers and their families.

real: A monetary unit of silver. Eight reales make a peso. A real is equivalent to twelve granos.

reata: A braided leather lasso.

reduction: A mission or the process of missionization. The state of affairs resulting from the indigenous people's being grouped together closely at and around the missions.

regidor: A member of the ayuntamiento or town council.

reglamento: Regulation or proclamation.

sacristan: An individual having charge of the sacristy of the church, where vestments and various church accoutrements are kept to conduct religious services.

siliyik: A Chumash sacred area found within a village.

Surf: Where the Santa Ynez River meets the sea in the Lompoc Valley.

tasajo: A Spanish term for jerked beef, which was used extensively at the missions.

temescal: A Chumash sweat lodge.

testigo: A wedding witness. Often, certain neophyte testigos were called upon to witness a whole series of sequential marriages on a given occasion.

tomol: A kind of Chumash canoe made out of wood planks.

tules, tular: The swamp area of the Central Valley; the abode of both runaway and gentile Indians. Some refugees from the 1824 revolt retreated to the region of the Tulares, an area known as San Emigdio Rancho near Buenavista Lake.

vaquero: A cowboy or expert horseman.

vara: Spanish yard of about 33 inches. It was equivalent to 2.7424 feet in colonial California.

viña: Another term for vineyard.

wot: A Chumash village leader

ynterprete: An interpreter who aided the priest in preaching to the Indians.

zanja: The Spanish name for a ditch used for irrigation.

Timeline of Building Construction at La Purísima Mission

1788: Temporary structures of palisade or adobe with roofs of packed earth were built. This included a chapel, quarters for the missionaries, a granary, two corrals and two rooms for which a use was not specified. Cota stated in August 1788 that there were five gente de razón families at the mission and he had sent for two more.

1789: A church, granary and common kitchen were built of adobe. This was the first permanent church at Mission Vieja. It was made of adobe with a flat roof covered with straw and earth. It was about seventeen feet wide and sixty-two feet long. The sacristy of the church was seventeen feet wide and sixteen and a half feet long. The sacristy was where vestments and other accoutrements of the church were stored.

1790: A wing with seven rooms of adobe was added to the growing complex. A kiln was built to fire roof tiles. After 1790, buildings were constructed of adobe with tile roofs.

1791: A granary of adobe was built as part of the main quadrangle, and three buildings were erected outside the quadrangle: a kitchen, an oven and a chicken coop.

1792: The mission was badly damaged by floods. The adobe church and a granary were renovated.

1793: An adobe wing containing new quarters for the missionaries, apartments for visitors, an office, a storage room for Indian clothing and a kitchen were added to the main quadrangle.

1794: New quarters for soldier guards were built. This building was about thirty-eight feet in length and seventeen feet wide. A room for the mayordomo was added, as was a warehouse for various goods and implements. A carpenter shop was built, and a tack room for the outfits of pack animals was constructed. All these buildings were of adobe and roofed with tiles. Lastly, a corridor of brick was added to the main building.

1795: In this year, they began to collect materials for a more permanent church, the foundations of which were laid in 1798. A vaulted granary was constructed, and another room of equal size contiguous to it was built and roofed with tiles.

1796: Three capacious apartments for keeping implements were constructed. Various other structures were repaired or renovated.

1797: A new residence building (more suitable habitations) was built for the missionaries.

1798: A new guardhouse was erected for the soldiers. Nine houses were built for as many convert Indian families. This number was to grow to one hundred housing units for Indian families that were to become unusable after the earthquake of 1812. Another storehouse was constructed, and the foundations for a larger church were laid without the help of a master builder. All new structures were of adobe and were roofed with tiles.

1799: Additions were made to the main building. Two buildings each ten varas (or about twenty-seven feet) long were constructed of adobe and roofed with tiles.

1800: Another wing was added to the mission of adobe and roofed with tiles. The wing was divided up into eight rooms and was 70 varas (192 feet) long and 7 varas (19 feet) wide.

APPENDIX 1

1802: The adobe church begun in 1798 was completed. It was most likely dedicated on December 8, 1802, the anniversary of the founding of the mission. During this year, the garden, which was about two hundred yards square, was surrounded by a single adobe wall.

1804: A guardhouse and five dwellings with as many kitchens, one for each soldier family, were built. These included a good patio. The whole structure was forty yards long.

1808: Payeras reported that the rancho at Salsipuedes was being provided with irrigation and it was predicted that it would soon be productive.

1810: During the winter of 1809–10, an old building was renovated by tiling the roof and whitewashing the walls. This was at the Reyes Rancho. Also, work was done to improve the flow of water there. A granary and house were also built at Rancho San Antonio north of the mission. In order to facilitate travel for the public and mail carriers and to shorten the distance from Mission Santa Inés to La Purísima and from La Purísima to Mission San Luis Obispo, two roads were opened through the mountains of the Santa Ynez River. The roads were one league (two and a half to three miles) apart, and each road was forty paces wide.

1812: Earthquake activity was first felt at Mission La Purísima on December 8 with slight shocks in the morning. Little damage was done. Nearly two weeks later, the earth began to shake with disastrous results. The church and vestry that had been completed in 1802 were completely destroyed. Some of the workshops went down. One hundred houses of neophyte Indians and the pozolera, or community kitchen, became unserviceable. The garden wall constructed in 1802 went down. Following the earthquake, heavy rains created further damage, causing destruction to mission waterworks. A temporary church of palisades was constructed, along with two huts of poles and grass to serve as habitations for the padres.

1813: In April 1813, the mission moved to a new site several miles away across the Santa Ynez River. The Chumash word for the second site of La Purísima (where the state park is today) was Amúu. It was not a village. The Chumash word referred to a type of plant that grew at the location. The site was located in La Cañada de los Berros (Valley of the Watercress) and was noted for beautiful California wildflowers. Within nine months' time, a church had been constructed of poles veneered with adobes. This structure was roofed with tile (most likely recovered from the first mission site). The church was an adequate size to hold all the necessary people. In order to maintain the mission with water independent of the Santa Ynez River, a small fountain was built from which a ditch conducted water to the foot of the mission for a distance of four hundred paces. To secure a greater volume of water for summer irrigation, an aqueduct that ran from the river to the old mission site was continued to the new mission site, crossing the river at the old pass of Santa Ynez. An orchard was planted with as many trees as were at hand, and these were irrigated with water from various springs that was collected after emptying into tanks. While the date of construction of the first permanent Indian housing is not known, it has been suggested that this occurred as early as 1813.

1814: According to the Mission Account Book, in 1813 and 1814, sawyers were cutting and stockpiling pine and poplar to cure with the intent of using it two years hence. Some logs were raw, and others were dressed. Pines were cut for a stockade on the site of Los Pinos beyond La Graciosa. Pine for stockade poles was also obtained in the small range of mountains of La Cuesta. Timber was obtained from the Santa Lucia Mountains for construction of buildings. Lumber was also obtained from an area along the Alamo River. This wood was poplar, some of which was to be used for axles and cart poles.

1815: Indians were making adobes with which to build a guardhouse, storehouse and soldiers' dwellings. The church was reinforced and plastered. A large building some 277 feet in length and 166 feet wide was started. It was divided down the center of its long axis to form apartments oriented to both sides. These provided residences for the ministers, rooms for servants and guests, a workshop and a chapel. One side had a covered corridor and the other a walk. By October of that year, ministers were living in their new rooms.

1816: Another large adobe structure was built of the same size and division. Corridors on both sides afforded access to the guardroom, barracks, an apartment for the mayordomo and the carpentry and weaving shops. The chapel was decorated (residence building), and two infirmaries were constructed.

Appendix 1

1817: The church of 1813 was repaired, and foundations were prepared for a new one. A fountain with a lavatory was located between the apartments of the padres and the houses of the Spanish families. Another fountain was provided for the Indians. A hostelry for travelers, built of palisades and tules, was erected at Rancho de Larga.

1818: In September of this year, a fire destroyed almost all the houses of the neophytes, and it took a year to replace them. The temporary church built in 1813 collapsed and was replaced by a new temporary church built of adobe. The church completed in 1818 may have been built on the foundations laid the previous year.

1821: A bell tower was added to the church.

1822: The only windmill to have been built in colonial California was begun on December 25 by Ferencio Ruiz. No record was made of its completion, however.

1823: Ten new houses with tile roofs were provided for neophytes.

1825: As a result of the Indian uprising at La Purísima, the church was damaged to the extent that it had to be replaced. A new one was dedicated on October 4, 1825.

1835: The chapel in the building constructed in 1815 was renovated because the church completed in 1818 was in poor condition. The renovated chapel served for the reduced Indian population.

Sources: Construction chronologies were particularly useful from the following: Jackson, *Missions and the Frontiers of Spanish America*, 434–35; Hardwick, "Founding of Mission La Purísima Concepción," 9–10; Englehardt, *Mission La Concepción Purísima de María Santísima*, 8–12; Neuerburg, *Architecture of Mission La Purísima Concepción*; and Schuetz-Miller, *Building and Builders in Hispanic California*, 196–98.

ESCOLTA (SOLDIER GUARD) ASSIGNED TO MISSION LA PURÍSIMA

1789: *Sergeant José María Ortega*, of the mission guard
Wife: Francisca Lopez (Bap Gente de Razón #110)

1790: *Sergeant José María Ortega*, in charge of mission guard
Wife: Francisca (Bap Gente de Razón #278)
Francisco de Paula Garcia, leather jacket soldier of the mission guard (native of Villa de Puente Real, Andalucia, Spain)
Wife: María Luisa Ortega (Bap Gente de Razón #171)
Juan Romero, leather jacket soldier of the mission guard
Wife: María Lugardo Salgado (Bap Gente de Razón #279)
Luis Romero, leather jacket of the mission guard: padrino
Wife: María Germana Gómez (Bap Gente de Razón #279)
Anastasio Feliz, soldier of this garrison
Wife: María Gertrudes Valenzuela (Soldier Garrison)
Ignacio Lugo, soldier of this garrison
Wife: Mariana Gertrudes Limón (Soldier Garrison)
Hilario Ximenez, soldier of the garrison
Wife: Indian woman, neophyte of Santa Bárbara Mission (Soldier Garrison)
Lamberto (Indian Juan of Old California), Soldier Garrison
Juan Melchor López, soldier of the garrison

APPENDIX 2

1791: *Hilario Ximenez*, leather jacket soldier
  Wife: Juana, Indita, neophyte of Purísima (Purísima 1ˢᵗ Confirm #352)

1794: *Corporal Francisco Xavier Albarado*, corporal of this garrison
  Wife: María Ygnacia Amador (Soldier Garrison)

1795: *Corporal Francisco Xavier Albarado*, corporal of the guard (padrino)
  Wife: María Ygnacia Amador (Purísima 1ˢᵗ Confirm #890)

1797: *Sergeant Ygnacio Olivera*
  Wife: Marcela Feliz (Easter Duty)
  Manuel Ygnacio Lugo, soldier (refer to 1790)
    Wife: Gertrudes Limón (Easter Duty)
  Clemente Navarro, soldier
    Wife: María del Carmen Rochin (Easter Duty)
  Francisco Solorzano, soldier
    Wife: Faustina Lara (Easter Duty)
  José de la Cruz Bermúdez, soldier (refer to 1812 census)
    Wife: María Estefana Villa (Easter Duty)
  Antonio María Lugo, soldier
    Wife: Maía Dolores Ruiz (Easter Duty)
  Maximo Piña (single man) (Easter Duty)
  Xavier Pico (single man) (Easter Duty)

1800: *Joseph Cristoval Palomaros*, listed as cabo (corporal) of the guard of the mission and native of Real de San Joseph de Canelas (Bap Gente de Razón #1315)

1813: *Corporal Vicente Villa*, listed as corporal of the guard who mutually decided with the mission neophytes to relocate the mission to the Berros Canyon site.
  Wife: Rita Valdéz, native of La Purísima (Payeras Letter, 1813)

1818: Father Payeras lists the mission escolta as follows:
  Corporal Villa
  Secundio Olivera
  Ygnacio Yguera [Higuera]
  Eustaquio Peña
  Manuel Germán
  José Antonio Ortega (Writings of Mariano Payeras)

1820: Easter Duty list for April 24, 1820, lists the mission guard as follows:
Corporal Tiburcio Tapia
Secundio Olivera, soldier
   Wife: María Antonia Stuard
Sefarino Carlon, soldier and son of *Felipe de Goicoechea*, Santa Bárbara Presidio comandante (1784–1802)
   Wife: Dominga Cota
Vicente Feliz (soldier)
Gabriel Garcia (soldier)

1822: Payeras stated that six soldiers composed the escolta guard of the mission. He felt that this would hardly be enough soldiers in case of an emergency; consequently, Payeras proposed a rather elaborate plan to form an Indian militia at the mission.

1824: Account of the mission revolt (February 1824) lists *Corporal Tiburcio Tapia* with his four or five men (escolta) as defenders of the mission during the night until his powder runs out. He subsequently surrenders and travels to Mission Santa Inés with Padre Ordáz to prevent Sergeant Anastasio Carrillo from coming with his troops and thus causing slaughter of families at La Purísima. (Bancroft)

1825: La Purísima Account Book lists the following individuals drawing rations for the guardhouse:
Sergeant Damaso Rodríguez

1826: *José Manual Cota*, listed as corporal of the guard at La Purísima Mission
Juan Alvarez, soldier (Bap Gente de Razón #3176)

1828: La Purísima Account Book lists the following soldiers of the guard who received cattle from the mission in 1828:
Sergeant Juan Salazar
Corporal Carlos Ruiz
José Antonio Ortega, soldier
   Wife: Secundia Cordero, native of this province (Bap Gente de Razón #3193)
Francisco Garcia, soldier of the guard
Luciano Félix
Vicente Félix

APPENDIX 2

Thomas Garcia
Ramon Valdés
Joaquín Villa
Juan María Olivera
Juan Cordero

Sources: "Bap Gente de Razón" refers to Baptismal Records of the Gente de Razón of La Purísima Mission (numbers refer to record entries). "Soldier Garrison" are "Soldier of the Garrison Entries" found in the first book of confirmations for the mission. "Purisima 1ˢᵗ Confirm" refers to First Book of Confirmations for Mission La Purísima. "Easter Duty" refers to manuscript file #57 in the La Purísima Mission Archives. Census and Easter Duty lists from the originals in the Bancroft Library translated by Thomas Workman Temple. A copy of the translation was received from William Mason, archivist, L.A. County Museum. There are lists of names for the years 1797, 1812 and 1820. "Payeras Letter, 1813," comes from a letter by Mariano Payeras and Antonio Ripoll (March 11, 1813) to Father President Señan requesting the removal of La Purísima to a new site after the earthquake of 1812. The letter was filed in the Bancroft Library in 1877 and is also on file in Santa Barbara Mission Archive Library, vol. 6, Misc. Papers, 166–77. Cutter, *Writings of Mariano Payeras*, 153. "Bancroft" refers to *History of California, vol. II, 1801–1824*, 529.

SIGNIFICANT INDIAN VILLAGES OF THE LA PURÍSIMA AREA

Algascupi (Alagsakupi) is the Spanish name for the Chumash: *laxshakupi/ 'alaxshakupi.* In Chumash, the word perhaps means "quick." This was the place name for the original site of Mission La Purísima currently in the town of Lompoc. According to John Johnson of the Santa Bárbara Natural History Museum, the location was not an occupied village at the time the mission was established. Lompo' apparently was the occupied village and appears on his map, *Chumash Towns at the Time of European Settlement.*

Amúu ('Amuwu) is the Chumash word for the second site of La Purísima (where the state park is today). It was not a village. The Chumash word refers to a type of plant that grew at the location. The site was located in La Cañada de los Berros (Valley of the Watercress) and was noted for beautiful California wildflowers.

Bulito/Estayt/Kashtayit (near Gaviota) village was located at Cañada de Santa Anita, west of Gaviota. It provided 107 baptisms listed in Mission La Purísima records (Brown, "Aboriginal Population," 95). This village is one of the top three villages whose inhabitants were baptized at the mission. Between Bultio and Cojo was a small village called Santa Anita/Texax. In 1769, Juan Crespí counted some twenty houses that were allegedly on the seashore, where it was wide and spacious. In 1796, the village population was estimated to be about thirty inhabitants. The village provided 52 baptisms to Mission La Purísima (Brown, "Aboriginal Population," 95).

Cojo (Sisolop)/Shisholop is just below Point Concepción at El Cojo. At times, the Spanish referred to the village as Santa Teresa. In early August 1772, José de Cañizares, master of a Spanish ship, anchored under Point Concepción and found the "the first heathen village to be seen" to bear east-northeast from what is now Government Point. Ships found a watering place beside the village. Spanish explorers estimated the village population to be over one hundred at various times living in numerous large grass houses. Explorers noted also the presence of canoes at the village site. In 1796, Goycoechea from the presidio of Santa Bárbara estimated the village population to be seventy-two and named the chief of the village, Cuyayamahuit. This was the same man, Puyayemehuit (MLP Baptism 1209), listed as Capitán de Sisolop, whose son was baptized on October 29, 1798. Mission La Purísima recorded 158 baptisms from Cojo (Brown, "Aboriginal Population," 95), making this one of the top three Indian villages listed in the mission records for recorded baptisms. The mission also used Cojo as an anchorage for trading ships.

Espada/Shilimaqshtush was a typical Purismeño village that the Spanish named Espada. The village got its Spanish name from an incident that occurred during the Portolá expedition of 1769 when an Indian tried to steal a soldier's sword. It was located where Jalama County Park is now. Shilimaqshtush was a medium-sized village. In 1769, the Portolá expedition estimated that between 140 and 200 people lived in the village, which consisted of between twenty and thirty houses. A total of 106 baptisms were recorded in the missions from this village; 98 of them were at Mission La Purísima (94 according to Brown, , "Aboriginal Population," 95), and 8 were recorded at Mission San Luis Obispo. No canoes were observed at the village by various explorers. The people of the village obtained most of the plants, animals and other resources they needed within less than a half-day walk from the village. There was also a village called Halam (Jalama) on what is now Jalama Creek east of Point Concepción. This village was located inland from what is now Jalama County Park.

Gaviota/Nomgio/Onomyo was a large Chumash population center. In 1769, journals describe the town ranging on both banks of the inlet or estuary that once covered the floor of the Gaviota Creek Valley. Juan Crespí with the expedition noted people in swarms numbering nearly three hundred "heathens." Some fifty-two large houses were counted with approximately seven canoes associated with the village. Mission La Purísima baptized the largest number of neophytes (159) from Gaviota (Brown, "Aboriginal Population," 95).

Itiax (Ytias Creek on the San Julian Ranch)

Jojonnta/Xonxon'ata, near Ballard, means sixteen lodges.

Kesmalia

Lompo' was an occupied Chumash village at the time of Spanish contact. Its meaning is "stagnant or brackish water," and it is most likely where the town of Lompoc got its name. The village was located adjacent to the Santa Ynez River not far inland from Surf where the Santa Ynez River meets the sea, close to the mouth of Lompoc Canyon and the entrance of South Vandenberg Air Force Base. The village was first observed in May 1770 while soldiers were looking for a way to ford the Santa Ynez River. Padre Juan Crespí, the journalist of the expedition, noted: "At this spot there are a great many bears, for there are a great many of their tracks throughout the dunes here. The soldiers who went seeking a ford, and failed to find one [within] about a league from the shore, did come across a good-sized village of very fine heathens having about twenty-some large grass houses like those on the Channel."

Lospe (near Point Sal)

Lououato was a Yokuts village name, not Chumash. Only one individual was baptized from this village, and he is listed as a Yokuts Indian in later records.

Mikiw (Dos Pueblos Canyon) in Barbareño territory

Pedernales/Noqto was the last regular town of the channel, according to Juan Crespí in 1769. The town was described as a small-sized village (sixty to one hundred well-behaved "heathens"). Miguel Costansó, engineer on the Portolá expedition of 1769, mentioned a narrow point near the town covered with flint stones. The town was, therefore, named by the Spanish *Pedernales*. It was located on a creek near Point Arguello. Mission La Purísima baptized fifty-seven Indians from this village (Brown, "Aboriginal Population," 95).

A map of Chumash towns along the central coast. Some spellings and names of villages vary according to ethnographic records. *Map by Sally McLendon and John Johnson, 1999.*

FIGURE 3.1

Chumash Towns
at the time of
European Settlement

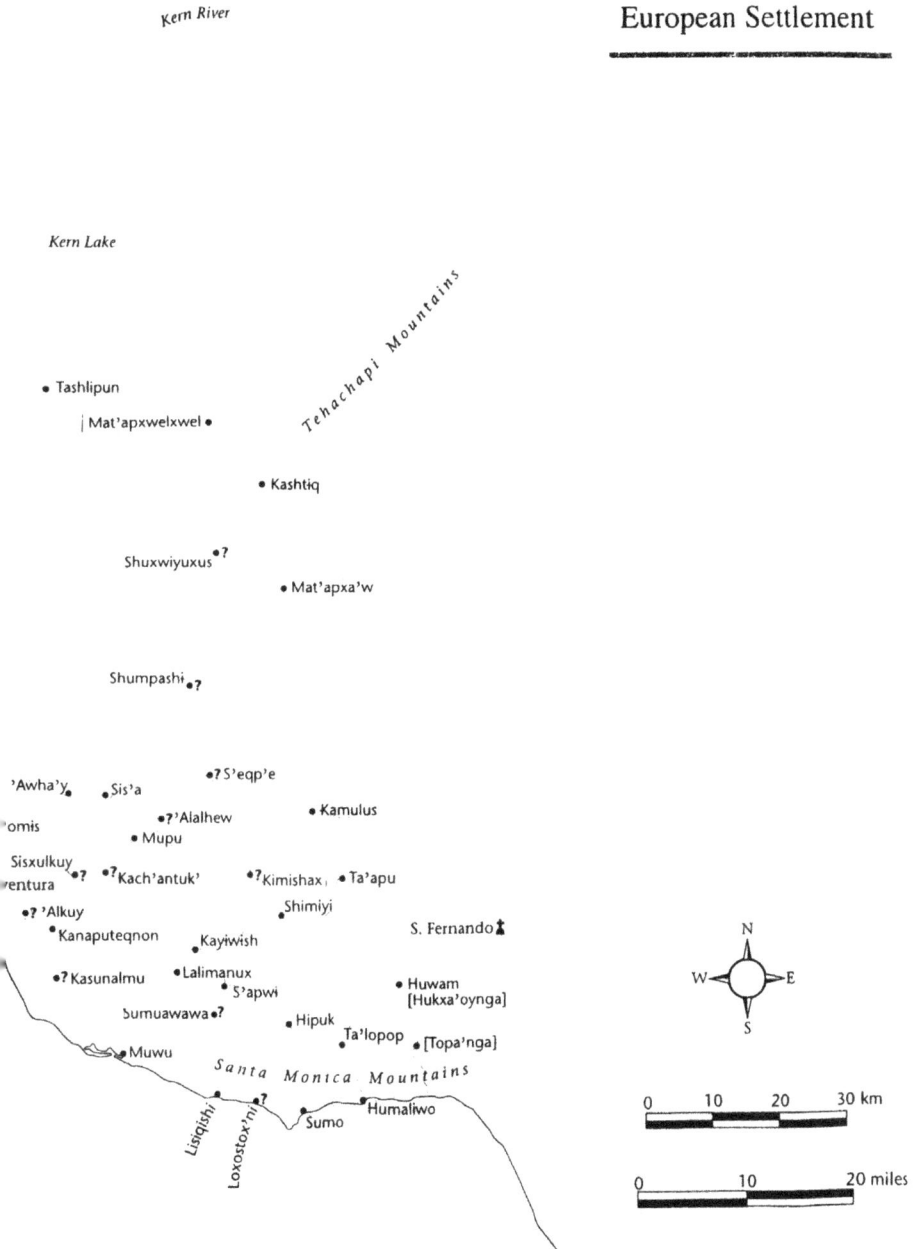

Kern River

Kern Lake

Tehachapi Mountains

• Tashlipun

| Mat'apxwelxwel •

• Kashtiq

Shuxwiyuxus •?

• Mat'apxa'w

Shumpashi •?

•? S'eqp'e

'Awha'y•   • Sis'a

•omis   •?'Alalhew   • Kamulus
          • Mupu

Sisxulkuy•?   •?Kach'antuk'   •?Kimishax, • Ta'apu
•entura
•? 'Alkuy   •Shimiyi
• Kanaputeqnon   • Kayïwish   S. Fernando ⚑

•? Kasunalmu   • Lalimanux
                    • S'apwï   • Huwam
Sumuawawa •?   [Hukxa'oynga]
          • Muwu   • Hipuk
                    • Ta'lopop • [Topa'nga]

Santa Monica Mountains

Lisiqishï   Loxostox'nï
          •?   • Humaliwo
          • Sumo

N
W — ⊕ — E
S

0   10   20   30 km

0   10   20 miles

Quemada/Shisuch'i' as a village was not originally noticed in the Spanish expeditions of 1769–70. The Spanish name *Quemada* means burnt village, but it is not known how the name was originally associated with the village. It was located on the height of a bluff very close to shore near Quemada Canyon about halfway between what is now El Capitán and Gaviota just before Arroyo Hondo. In 1796, the village had 250 souls, the largest number of any channel town for this date. (Brown, "Aboriginal Population," 23). Mission La Purísima baptized forty Indians from this village (Brown, "Aboriginal Population," 95).

Santa Rosa/Sh'ahuchu is a village that was on Santa Rosa Ranch east of Lompoc. Estimates of village size are one hundred or more. Santa Rosa holds the distinction of being the residence of the first Indian listed in the Purísima baptismal record on April 9, 1788. The convert was twenty-two years old and named Matisaquit. He adopted the baptismal name of Francisco de la Concepción (Englehardt, *Mission La Concepción Purísima de María Santísima*, 7).

Saxpil/S'axpilil (near Casmalia)

Tsikyiw, near Avila in Obispeño territory.

Sources: The map "Chumash Towns at the Time of European Settlement," edited by McLendon and Johnson (*Cultural Affiliation*), was useful in identifying Chumash place names. Personal communication with anthropologist John Johnson from the Santa Bárbara Museum of Natural History helped to clarify some of the finer points regarding various villages. Brown, "Aboriginal Population," is a source of detailed information on the aboriginal population of the Santa Barbara Channel.

CULTIVATED CROPS GROWN AT MISSION LA PURÍSIMA

Production of foodstuffs was a first concern of the upper California mission padres. Cultivated crops, gardens, orchards and vineyards yielded most of the basic foodstuffs, along with meat and fats from cattle and sheep. The following compilation identifies crops grown at La Purísima, as mentioned in the mission records and compiled by the National Park Service in 1941.

CULTIVATED CROPS

REGULARLY REPORTED	OCCASIONALLY REPORTED
Barley (coast barley)	Horse beans
Beans (*Phaseolus vulgaris*)	
Red beans, white beans, lima beans	Pulse or lentils
Corn	Oats
Peas (pisium, chicharo, garbanzo)	
Wheat (propo, a bearded sort, little club)	

HORTICULTURE

LA PURÍSIMA	OTHER MISSIONS
Almonds	Apples
Apples (perones?)	Apricots
Grapes	Atron

La Purísima	Other Missions
Olives	Bananas
Pears	Dates
Pepper trees	Figs
	Kapolini (cherry)
	Lemons
	Oranges
	Peaches
	Pears
	Peppers
	Plums
	Pomegranates

VEGETABLES AND GARDEN

La Purísima	Other Missions
Cabbage	Onion
Chilies	Potatoes
Garlic	Radish
Mint	Watermelons

MISCELLANEOUS CROPS

La Purísima	Other Missions
Cotton	Tobacco
Flax	Plantain
Hemp	Coconuts
Indigo	Sugarcane

Sources: The compilation of crops grown at Mission La Purísima are from an "Outline of Agriculture" by Olaf Hagen, regional supervisor of historic sites, Region Four, National Parks Service, San Francisco, 1941.

SOURCES OF PLANTS FOR RESTORATION OF MISSION LA PURÍSIMA

When La Purísima Mission was reconstructed in the 1930s, much thought was given to the mission garden. Ed Rowe was given the task of bringing it to life. He was rigorous in collecting plants that were introduced into California during the mission days. He obtained reproductive stock from original plants still growing at or near the missions and at some of the old ranchos. An account of the original plants is included below.

PLANT NAME	SOURCE
Acacia farnesiana	Cave Couts' Rancho
Artichokes	Near Mission Santa Inés
Arundo donax	A giant reed of southern Europe and Asia Minor that was used for roofing purposes. At Mission San Luis Obispo is an original ceiling in one of the rooms where arundo canes lashed with rawhide acted as a lath to hold the plaster. In 1852, there were eight acres of this reed growing in one place in Los Angeles.
Cactus (tuna)	Originally from Mexico
Castilian rose	Mission San Antonio

PLANT NAME	SOURCE
Cherry (Kapolini)	Ortega Rancho at Arroyo Hondo. At Arroyo Hondo, the old home of the Ortegas near Gaviota, were three very large trees of a variety of cherry, a native of the mountains of Central Mexico. They were known as Kapolini, and the trees were of considerable age. M.E. O'Niel remembered them as large trees when he was a boy some sixty years ago (before 1939). Seedlings from these trees were doing well at La Purísima.
China berry tree	From Asia originally. Seeds were probably used to make rosaries.
Datura (Angel's Trumpet)	
Fig tree	Mission Santa Clara (trees were started from an old tree found growing at the mission).
Grapes	Jalama. In Jalama Canyon, nearer the ocean than the pears, the mission fathers grew wine grapes. The remains of an old wine vat were still visible in the 1930s. From cuttings of grapevines that survived here were started the grapes that border the restored La Purísima mission garden.
Jasminum officinale	Juan Dana home at Nipomo. H.V. Smith in 1939 noted at the Don Juan Dana house at Nipomo is a pomegranate that is a small tree. There are a number of old pears at the same place. Here, too, I found a large plant of a variety of jasmine seldom cultivated today.
Lemon verbena	
Myrtus communis	Mission Santa Bárbara
Oleander, white	Shrub in Pío Pico's garden, twice removed. Chas. Francis Saunders, well-known author, donated cuttings of white oleander. The cuttings came from a plant that used to be at Mission San Juan Capistrano. The original plant grew in the garden of Pío Pico, the last Mexican governor of California.

PLANT NAME	SOURCE
Olive trees	Presented by A.M. Boyd of Santa Bárbara. Twenty-seven fifty-year-old trees from Boyd's Los Olivos orchard. The trees were originally planted as cuttings from Mission Santa Bárbara. Planting pieces about two feet long, one to two inches in diameter, started them.
Peaches	From seeds obtained from Cañón de Chelly and Oraibi. This variety dated back to Spanish times, perhaps to the first Jesuit missionaries in that area.
Pears	Cuttings from original trees at Missions San Juan Capistrano, La Purísima, San Juan Bautista, Santa Inés, San Luis Obispo and Carmel were grafted on seedling pear stock. Pear is an early introduction and was most probably grown from seed. In 1939, Ed Rowe stated that some pear trees exist at San Rafael, but the mission is gone. San Juan Bautista had the largest remaining number of any mission. On the plain below and north of the church stood the remains of an old orchard. In the orchard, some thirty trees were still standing. At Carmel, there were six in 1935. A number survived in the vicinity of Santa Inés. In the old orchard at San Antonio de Padua there were two healthy trees. At San Juan Capistrano, a large tree stood near the Santa Fe Rail Road station where the valley opens to the sea. At La Purísima, there was a large pear orchard just north of the mission buildings. One tree survived from this orchard. At Jalama, three great pear trees were still growing.
Pomegranate	Mission San Antonio and Juan Dana home. At San Antonio were found bushes of pomegranates. This plant is a native of northern Africa and western Asia. The plant was an early introduction and of considerable economic value. The juicy pulp is very refreshing. A red dye is made from the flowers, and the tough shell of the fruit contains tannic acid used for dyeing and tanning soft leathers. Cuttings from plants at San Antonio were used at La Purísima.

PLANT NAME	SOURCE
Prunus capolin	Ortega Rancho
Rue	This herb was originally found to be growing under the fig at Mission Santa Clara.
Seedling oranges	Indian orchard near the old San Marcos Pass. Old seedling orange trees at the Indian orchard in Goleta near the old San Marcos Pass were planted in Spanish times.

Sources: Rowe, "Report of the Gardens" and "Introduced Plants," is the source of original plants still growing at the missions and at some of the old ranchos. Weber, *Our Lady's Mission*, 153, is the source for mission pears that were obtained by Ed Rowe. Smith, paper, provided information on seedling orange trees in Goleta in the Old Indian Orchard near San Marcos Pass.

CHAPTER SOURCES

CHAPTER 1: MISSIONS AS FRONTIER SETTLEMENTS
The first four chapters of Sunset Books' *California Missions*, 8–47, provided good overviews of the California mission system. Especially useful was the chapter entitled "The Meaning of the Missions." John Johnson from Santa Bárbara Museum of Natural History (personal communication) confirmed that some twenty-five different Indian languages were spoken in California between Sonoma and San Diego. Williams and Davis, *Soldiers and Their Families*, 37–38, was a source of general information on escoltas at the missions.

CHAPTER 2: SPANISH BEGINNINGS IN THE LOMPOC VALLEY
Neve's report to the viceroy is to be found in Beilhartz, *Felipe de Neve*, 112. Brown, "Aboriginal Population," 449, gives the Crespí account of the beginnings of a name for Mission La Purísima. Englehardt, *Mission La Concepción Purísima*, provides basic founding information and commentary on the patroness of the mission, Purísima Concepción. Reference to a 1930 newspaper article about Indians named María may be found in abstract of article in Hardwick, "La Purísima Mission State Historic Park Archives," 46.

CHAPTER 3: CHUMASH OF THE LA PURÍSIMA AREA
Pedro Font's accounts of the Chumash are from Bolton, *Anza's California Expeditions*, 361–66. Village names both here and in the appendix were checked against material supplied by John Johnson. Johnson confirms that the Chumash spoke distinct regional languages and not dialects. Particularly useful was a map (McLendon and

Johnson, *Cultural Affiliation*) entitled "Chumash Towns at the Time of European Settlement." The La Purísima Mission Docent Training Manual provided specific information about Purismeño territory and specifics regarding the village of Shilimaqshtush. Blackburn, "Chumash Revolt of 1824," and Williams, *Chumash of California*, provided useful overview information of Chumash culture.

CHAPTER 4: THE FOUNDING OF LA PURÍSIMA CONCEPCIÓN
The spring 1975 issue of *Noticias* from the Santa Bárbara Historical Society is a source of information on the founding of La Purísima. Information on Pablo Cota is to be found in Powell, *Antepasados*. Neuerburg, *Architecture of Mission La Purísima*, provided much of the information on early artwork adorning the mission. Kristina Wilkinson Foss, museum director of Old Mission Santa Bárbara, compiled the art information from Neuerburg and helped define the art in Nuremburg's work. Information concerning La Purísima Rancho was obtained from *diseños* and land confirmation maps on file, call numbers E-44, E-45, E-46, in the Santa Barbara Mission Archive Library. The ruins of Mission Vieja as seen in the 1880s are described in Thompson and West, *History of Santa Barbara*, 30–31. Cutter, *Writings of Mariano Payeras*, 66–72, provides a good comparison between the old and new mission sites.

CHAPTER 5: NEOPHYTES AND FRANCISCANS
Englehardt, *Mission La Concepción Purísima*, 95–98, provided the basic list of padres serving at the mission at various times. Englehardt, *Mission La Concepción Purísima*, 81, is the source of Lasuén being the last father president to confirm at La Purísima. Geiger, *Franciscan Missionaries*, gave good biographical sketches of most of these padres. Bancroft, *California Pioneer Register*, 372, provided information on Father Victoria. Specific information on Father Arroyo de la Cuesta was found in Geiger, *Franciscan Missionaries*, 18–24. Ord, *California Recollections*, 64, and Bancroft, *Works of Bancroft, Vol. 2*, 489, provided additional information on Father Mariano Payeras.

CHAPTER 6: ECONOMICS OF THE MISSION
Englehardt, *Mission La Concepción Purísima*, 26, is the source of quotes regarding livestock statistics for the year 1810, as well as trade and annual clothing for the Indians. Hageman and Ewing, *Archeological and Restoration Study*, 236–67, provided information on economic activity at the mission. Engbeck, *La Purísima Mission*, 5–6, is the source for "Trade and Outside Influences" at the mission.

CHAPTER SOURCES

CHAPTER 7: RANCHES, LANDS AND ROADS OF LA PURÍSIMA

Cutter, *Writings of Mariano Payeras*, 66–72, identifies mission holdings and relative locations of some of these. Englehardt, *Mission La Concepción Purísima*, 19–20, references the ranches of La Larga, Reyes and San Antonio. He also makes scattered references with respect to orchards, vineyards and other mission holdings. Schuetz-Miller, *Building and Builders*, 197, references the construction of a hostelry for travelers at La Larga in 1817. An 1854 map, call number E-41, plots the two vineyards associated with La Purísima. It was the source of vineyard sizes and definitely establishes two vineyards associated with the mission. Older, *California Missions*, 175–77, is a good source for ranchos attached to the mission, especially with respect to listing mission ranchos for the year 1834. Hageman and Ewing, *Archeological and Restoration Study*, 253, provided livestock statistics for the year 1814. Palmer, *Central Coast Continuum*, 1–13, is the source of the current location of mission ranches and information on trails and roads. Occasional references are made to ranches and lands in Hardwick, "Mission Account Book."

CHAPTER 8: INDIAN LIFE AT THE MISSION

Sandos, *Converting California*, describes Lasuén's practical approach to educating Indians. He also provided information on the development of music in the missions. Engbeck, *La Purísima Mission*, 3–11, is the source of information regarding sea otter hunting and trade and provided general information on Indian life at the mission during the early years, including weaving and the quantity of blankets manufactured over the years. Routine life at La Purísima and the Gregorio Fernández reply to Indian mistreatments is to be found in Hageman and Ewing, *Archeological and Restoration Study*, 244–46, and also in Englehardt, *Mission La Concepción Purísima*, 12–18. Farris and Johnson, "Prominent Indian Families," provided much of the information on the division of Indian labor at the mission, while Robinson, *Life in Santa Barbara*, 59–61, provided the account of Indian vaqueros at the cattle farm of "Guadaloupe." Hageman and Ewing, *Archeological and Restoration Study*, 256–58, is the source of information regarding the Indian militia at La Purísima. Hackel, *Children of Coyote*, 412–13, is the source of information on José Pacomio Pogui.

CHAPTER 9: INDIAN REVOLT AT THE CHANNEL MISSIONS

Although there are several accounts of the revolt at La Purísima, the one in Osio, *History of Alta California*, 55–70, is cited here. A native account of the revolt is available from Blackburn, "Chumash Revolt of 1824," 223–27. Information on Pacomio, Indian leader of the Purísima revolt, was obtained from Osio, *History of Alta California*, 270–71, n. 12, and also from Bancroft, *Works of Bancroft, Vol. 2*, 527.

Estrada's account is from Englehardt, *Mission La Concepción Purísima*, 51–52. De La Guerra's action at Mission Santa Bárbara where he stops battling the Indians to go to lunch is described in Thompson, *El Gran Capitán*, 83.

CHAPTER 10: SECULARIZATION OF MISSION LA PURÍSIMA
Secularization specifics are from Johnson, "Chumash Indians after Secularization." Farris and Johnson, "Prominent Indian Families," was a source of specific Chumash Indian material. Janssens's account of La Purísima is from Hardwick, "La Purísima Mission State Historic Park Archives," 46. Accounts of the smallpox epidemic of 1844 were obtained by personal communication with Farris and Johnson. Vallejo, *Memoirs of the Vallejos*, 51–53, gives a very descriptive account of how the epidemic decimated California native populations in 1837–39.

CHAPTER 11: LA PURÍSIMA MISSION GARDEN
Thompson and West, *History of Santa Barbara*, 282, is the source of the opening quote in the chapter. H.V. Smith provided information on seedling orange trees in Goleta in the Old Indian Orchard near San Marcos Pass. Weber, *Our Lady's Mission*, 153, is the source for mission pears that were obtained by Ed Rowe.

CHAPTER 12: RESTORATION OF MISSION LA PURÍSIMA
This is perhaps best described in Hageman and Ewing, *Archeological and Restoration Study*. Land acquisition is detailed in the *Union Oil Bulletin*. A description of the La Purísima Archival Collections is described in History Associates Incorporated, "Guide to the La Purisima Mission State Historic Park Collection."

BIBLIOGRAPHY

Applegate, Richard. "An Index of Chumash Place Names." *Papers on the Chumash*. San Luis Obispo County Archaeological Society. Paso Robles, CA: Roberts House of Printing, 1975.

Bancroft, Hubert Howe. *California Pioneer Register and Index 1542–1848*. Baltimore, MD: Clearfield Company Reprints and Remainders, 1990.

———. *The Works of Hubert Howe Bancroft: History of California*. Vol. 2, *1801–1824*. Facsimile reprint, Santa Barbara, CA: Wallace Hebberd, 1966.

———. *The Works of Hubert Howe Bancroft: History of California*. Vol. 3, *1825–1840*. Facsimile reprint, New York: Arno Press, in cooperation with McGraw-Hill Book Company, 1886.

Beilhartz, Edwin A. *Felipe de Neve: The First Governor of California*. San Francisco: California Historical Society, 1971.

Blackburn, Thomas C. "The Chumash Revolt of 1824: A Native Account." *Journal of California Anthropology* 2 (1975): 223–27.

———. *December's Child: A Book of Chumash Oral Narratives Collected by J.P. Harrington*. Berkeley: University of California Press, 1975.

Bolton, Herbert Eugene. *Anza's California Expeditions: An Outpost of Empire*. Vol. 1. Originally published by the Regents of the University of California, 1930. Reissued, New York: Russell & Russell, 1966.

Brown, Alan K. "The Aboriginal Population of the Santa Barbara Channel." *University of California Archaeological Survey* 69, University of California Archaeological Research Facility, Department of Anthropology, Berkeley (January 1967).

————, ed. and trans. *A Description of Distant Roads: Original Journals of the First Expedition in California, 1769–1770 by Juan Crespí.* San Diego, CA: San Diego State University Press, 2001.

Costello, Julia G. "Archaeological Survey of Mission Vieja de la Purísima." *Pacific Coast Archaeological Society Quarterly* 11, no. 2 (April 1975).

Cutter, Donald. *Writings of Mariano Payeras.* Santa Barbara, CA: Bellerohphon Books, 1995.

Docent Training Manual. "Chumash Culture." La Purísima Mission State Historic Park, Lompoc, CA, April 2002.

Engbeck, Joseph H., Jr. *La Purísima Mission State Historic Park.* State of California, Department of Parks and Recreation, California Office of State Printing, 86911-768, September 1974.

Englehardt, Father Zephyrin. *Mission La Concepción Purísima de María Santísima.* From the original 1932 publication. Santa Barbara, CA: McNally & Loftin, 1986.

Farris, Glenn J., and John R. Johnson. "Prominent Indian Families at Mission La Purísima Concepción as Identified in Baptismal, Marriage, and Burial Records." Occasional Paper Number 3, California Mission Studies Association (December 1999).

Geiger, Maynard, OFM. *Franciscan Missionaries in Hispanic California 1769– 1848: A Biographical Dictionary.* San Marino, CA: Huntington Library, 1969.

Glassow, Michael A., ed. "Archaeology on the Northern Channel Islands of California: Studies of Subsistence, Economics, and Social Organization." *Archives of California Prehistory* 34 (1993).

Hackel, Steven W. *Children of Coyote, Missionaries of Saint Francis, Indian-Spanish Relations in Colonial California, 1769–1850.* Omohundro Institute of Early American History and Culture. Chapel Hill: University of North Carolina Press, 2005.

Hageman, Fred C., and Russell C. Ewing. *An Archeological and Restoration Study of Mission La Purísima Concepción, Reports Written for the National Park Service.* Edited by Richard S. Whitehead. Santa Barbara, CA: Santa Barbara Trust for Historic Preservation, 1980.

Hagen, Olaf T. "Outline of Agriculture (Industries) and Crafts at La Purísima." August 7, 1941. On file at La Purísima Mission Archives and the author also has a copy. Hagen was regional supervisor of historic sites, Region Four, National Park Service, San Francisco.

Hardwick, Michael R. "Arms and Armament Presidios of California." Work in progress.

————. *Changes in Landscape: The Beginnings of Horticulture in the California Missions.* 2ⁿᵈ ed. Orange, CA: Paragon Agency Publishers, 2005.

————. "La Purísima Mission Account Book." Translated in the 1930s as part of the mission restoration at La Purísima Camp SP-29, Lompoc, California. A copy of this work was bound and indexed with the help of Margaret and Leroy Villa of Santa Barbara, 1980.

————. "La Purísima Mission State Historic Park Archives: An Experiment in Interpretation and Preservation." *La Purísima Mission* (Summer 1973).

Hardwick, Michael R., Kristina Wilkinson and Russell A. Ruiz. "The Founding of Mission La Purísima Concepción." *Noticias* 21, no. 1 (Spring 1975). Santa Barbara Historical Society.

Harrington, John P. *The Eye of the Flute: Chumash Traditional History and Ritual as Told by Fernando Librado Kitsepawit to John P. Harrington.* Edited with notes by Travis Hudson, Thomas Blackburn, Rosario Curletti and Janice Timbrook. Santa Barbara, CA: Santa Barbara Museum of Natural History, 1977.

History Associates Incorporated. "Guide to the La Purísima Mission State Historic Park Collection." La Purísima Mission State Historic Park, Lompoc, California. Processing supervised by History Associates Incorporated, 2003. Available as an Internet PDF download, www.parks. ca.gov/pages/1080/files/fa_513_001.pdf.

Jackson, Robert H. *Missions and the Frontiers of Spanish America.* Scottsdale, AZ: Pentacle Press, 2005.

Johnson, John R. "The Chumash Indians after Secularization." Santa Bárbara Museum of Natural History, California Mission Studies Association Keepsake, November 1995.

McLendon, Sally, and John R. Johnson, eds. *Cultural Affiliation and Lineal Descent of Chumash Peoples in the Channel Islands and the Santa Monica Mountains.* 2 vols. Report prepared for the Archeology and Ethnography Program, National Park Service, Washington, D.C., by the Santa Barbara Museum of Natural History and Hunter College, City University of New York, 1999.

Neuerburg, Norman. *The Architecture of Mission La Purísima Concepción.* Santa Barbara, CA: Bellerophon Books, 1987.

Older, Fremont. *California Missions and Their Romances.* New York: Tudor Publishing Co., 1945.

Ord, Angustias de la Guerra. *The California Recollections of Angustias de la Guerra Ord (Occurrences in Hispanic California).* As dictated by Angustias de la Guerra Ord to Thomas Savage in 1878. Bilingual edition. Giorgio Perissinotto, ed.,

Academy of Franciscan History in Collaboration with the Santa Barbara Trust for Historic Preservation, Washington, D.C., 2004.

Osio, Antonio María. *The History of Alta California: A Memoir of Mexican California*. Translated, edited and annotated by Rose Marie Beebe and Robert M. Senkewicz. Madison: University of Wisconsin Press, 1996.

Palmer, Kevin (Lex). *Central Coast Continuum: From Ranchos to Rockets, a Historic Overview for the Inventory and Evaluation of Historic Sites, Buildings, and Structures, Vandenberg Air Force Base, California*. Santa Maria, CA: BTG, Inc., 1999.

Powell, Luan Davis. *Antepasados, Volume III, Pablo Antonio Cota, Soldado de Cuera: Pasó por Aquí*. San Francisco: Los Californianos, 1978–79.

Robinson, Alfred. *Life in California*. Santa Barbara, CA: Peregrine Publishers, Inc., 1970.

Rowe, E.D., foreman La Purísima SP-29. "Introduced Plants Mentioned by E.D. Rowe in Correspondence, Radio Address and Various Reports Reproduced at La Purísima." On file in La Purísima Mission Archives.

———. "A Report of the Gardens and Palms at the Purísima Mission." La Purísima State Historical Monument, August 1939. On file in La Purísima Mission Archives.

Ruth, Clarence. *Survey of 50 Chumash Sites 1930–1967*. Lompoc, CA, 1967.

Sandos, James A. *Converting California, Indians and Franciscans in the Missions*. New Haven, CT: Yale University Press, 2004.

Savage, Christine E. *New Deal Adobe: The Civilian Conservation Corps and the Reconstruction of Mission La Purísima 1934–1942*. Santa Barbara, CA: Fithian Press, 1991.

Schuetz-Miller, Mardith K. *Building and Builders in Hispanic California 1769–1850*. Southwestern Mission Research Center, Tucson, Arizona. Santa Barbara, CA: Santa Barbara Trust for Historic Preservation, 1994.

Smith, H.V. A paper with no title regarding La Purísima Mission Gardens, 1939. It is on file in the La Purísima Mission Archives.

Sunset Books, Editorial Staff. *The California Missions: A Pictorial History*. Menlo Park, CA: Lane Book Company, 1971.

Thompson, Father Joseph A., OFM. *El Gran Capitán, José De la Guerra*. Los Angeles: Cabrera & Sons, 1961.

Thompson, Thomas H., and Albert Augustus West. *History of Santa Barbara and Ventura Counties, California*. 1883, reprinted Berkeley, CA: Howell-North, 1961.

Union Oil Bulletin 18, no. 10 (October 1937). Reprinted by the La Purísima Mission State Historic Park Advisory Committee, May 1978.

Vallejo. "Historical and Personal Memoirs" 2, no. 279 (n.d.).

Vallejo, Platon Mariano Guadalupe, MD. *Memoirs of the Vallejos*. Fairfield, CA: James D. Stevenson, Publisher, 1994.

Weber, Francis J., MSGR. *Our Lady's Mission: A Documentary History of La Purísima Concepción*. Hong Kong: Libra Press Limited, n.d.

Whitehead, Richard S., and Donald C. Cutter, eds. *Citadel on the Channel: The Royal Presidio of Santa Bárbara, Its Founding and Construction 1782–1798*. Santa Barbara, CA: Santa Barbara Trust for Historic Preservation and the Arthur H. Clark Company, 1996.

Wilkinson, S. Kristina, and Michael R. Hardwick. "The Founding of Mission La Purísima Concepción." *Noticias* 21, no. 1 (Spring 1975). Santa Barbara Historical Society.

————. "La Purísima: A Living Museum of Spanish Colonial History." *Noticias* 19, no. 2 (Summer 1973). Santa Barbara Historical Society.

Williams, Jack S. *The Chumash of California*. New York: PowerKids Press, Rosen Publishing Group, Inc., 2002.

Williams, Jack S., and Thomas L. Davis. *Soldiers and Their Families of the California Mission Frontier*. New York: PowerKids Press, Rosen Publishing Group, Inc., 2003.

INDEX

A

acorns 31
agriculture 14, 34, 40
alcalde 68, 74, 83, 85
alchuklash 85
Alemany, Bishop Alemany 87
Aleuts 55
Algascupi 18, 57, 115
Alta California 18, 35
Amúu 40, 107
antap 26
Anza 29
apostolado 38
Arguello 17, 25, 32
Argüello, Governor Dario 70, 76, 79
Arrillaga, Governor José Joaquín 40
Arroita, Father José 20, 45
arrows 68, 70, 72, 73, 77
Arroyo, Father Felipe Arroyo de la
    Cuesta 51
Arroyo Grande 25
artichokes 88
asistencia 60

atole 63
Avila 32

B

Baltazar, Indian musician 86
Barbareño 25, 32, 83
barley 52, 58, 59
barrio 83
bishop 44
blacksmiths 66
blankets 14, 46, 54, 65, 73
Book of Baptisms 45
Boscana, Father Gerónimo 48
Bouchard, Hippolyte de (Argentine
    insurgent) 47, 49, 67
Bulito/Kashtay't 25
Burton Mesa 61

C

Calluelas, Corporal (in charge of
    Macario road) 35
Calzada, Father José Antonio 46
Camino Real 41, 57, 59, 60

Canaliños 24
cannon 76, 78
carpenters 62, 66, 85
Carrillo, Domingo 83
Carrillo, Joaquín 42, 84
Carrillo, José Antonio Ezquiel 43, 84
Carrillo, Lieutenant Raimundo 54
Carrillos 87
Carrillo, Sergeant Carlos 67
Carrillo, Sergeant Don Anastasio 72
Casmalia 32, 57, 59, 60
Castilian rose 88, 123
cattle 34, 40, 47, 53, 56, 57, 58, 59,
    60, 64, 66, 80, 84
CCC (Civilian Conservation Corps)
    93, 94
Cecilio, Indian musician 86
Chase, Pearl 93
chia 31
choirs 62
Chumash 15, 24, 25, 26, 29, 32,
    34, 40, 46, 47, 49, 50, 55, 58,
    59, 61, 62, 63, 69, 80, 82, 83,
    85, 87, 107
cigars 54, 85, 86
clans, Chumash 25
cloth 14, 38, 46, 54, 64
Cojo Bay 58
Cojo/Shisholop 25
Confirmation 44
cooks 66, 85
corn 40, 52, 54, 57, 58, 59, 64, 65
cornucopias 38
corporal of the guard 64, 112
Cota, Sergeant Pablo Antonio (later
    alférez) 18, 35, 37, 60, 105
Cota, Valentín 70
cowboys 15, 66
Crespí, Fray Juan 17
crops 14, 15, 32, 35, 52, 57, 59, 64, 83

cueras 54, 72
Cuyama 25

D

de la Cuesta, Edwardo (purchased
    La Purísima, 1883) 87
de la Guerra y Noriega, Captain
    José (comandante del Presidio
    Santa Barbara) 67, 70, 75, 78
discipline 15
Dos Pueblos 25, 32

E

earthquake (1812) 7, 9, 38, 40, 44,
    45, 47, 89, 101, 106, 107
Echéandia, Governor José Maria
    82, 83, 101
economy 24, 56
Egorov, Prokhor (Indian instigator) 69
El Bulito Creek 29
Elceario 85, 86
Emigdiano 25
Enríquez, Antonio (weaver) 54
escolta 15, 18, 37, 68, 72, 112
Estrada, Lieutenant Don Mariano
    76, 77, 78

F

Fages, Governor Pedro 18, 35, 37
Fernández, Father Gregório 46, 63
Fernando, Librado 85
fiestas 24
fig trees 88
Figueroa, Governor José 83
firearms 32, 68, 74, 102
Font, Fray Pedro 26, 29
Fustér, Father Vicente 20, 45

G

ganado mayor (major livestock) 53
ganado menor (minor livestock) 53
Gaviota 25, 29, 58, 116
gente de razón 45, 54, 55, 70, 72,
    84, 105
Gil, Father Gil y Taboada 49
goats 53
godfathers 66
godmothers 66
Goicoechea, Comandante Felipe de
    37, 60, 63
Graciosa and Harris Canyons 60
granary 46, 58, 59, 105, 106, 107
Grant, Ulysses S. 43, 84
grapes 88
Guadalupe 58, 59, 60

H

hard labor 63, 80
Harrington, John P. 58, 70, 85
Harrington, Mark 93
Henriquez, Antonio 46
hide and tallow trade 56
Highway 1 61
historic gardening 89
Honda Canyon 58
Hora, Father (San Miguel) 63
Huerta Mateo 61

I

Iguala, Plan of 69
illicit trade 54
Immaculate Conception 17, 18, 38
Indian craftsmen 54
Indians 7, 14, 16, 18, 25, 29, 35,
    37, 40, 44, 45, 46, 47, 48, 49,
    50, 54, 55, 56, 62, 63, 64, 65,
    66, 69, 70, 72, 73, 74, 75, 76,

77, 78, 79, 80, 82, 83, 84,
    85, 86, 87, 89, 102, 103, 107,
    108, 109, 117, 120
California 14, 55, 99
Christianized 15
Chumash 11, 18, 56
female 20, 21
hostile 35, 74, 77
mission 15, 16, 34, 63, 65, 69, 70,
    82, 86, 97
native 14
neophyte 45, 63, 65
of Mexico 69
Santa Bárbara 28
unconverted 15
industries, mission 46, 65
Ineseño 25, 34
infirmary 67
instruments, musical 14, 62
interpreter 66, 104
irrigation 18, 52, 59, 65, 89, 104,
    107, 108
islay 31

J

jacales 28
Jalama 25, 31, 52, 57, 58, 60, 61,
    88, 89
Janssens, Señora Malo de 52, 86, 87

K

Kapolini cherry 88
Kesmalia 61, 117
Kroeber, Alfred 24

L

La Espada 25
La Larga 59
lances 67, 68, 77, 102

languages 14, 24, 62, 63
La Purísima Citizens Advisory
    Committee 92
La Purísima Hills 60
La Purísima Rancho 42, 84
Lasuén, Fray Fermín de 18, 44,
    48, 62
Laxshakupi 18
leather goods 54, 59
Librado, Fernando 58, 85, 86
Litany of All Saints 20
livestock 18, 34, 53, 57, 59, 80,
    82, 83
Lompoc 9, 18, 32, 37, 41, 47, 52,
    60, 89, 94
Lompoc Valley 17, 25, 35, 53
Los Alamos 58, 83, 84
Los Berros 10, 40, 43, 47, 59, 60,
    61, 65, 83, 107
Lospe 25, 32, 61, 117
Lououato 61
Luis el Cantor, Indian musician 86
lunette 38

M

Malo, Ramón 85, 86, 87
manual training 14
María 21, 86
Marquéz, Augustín (soldier from
    Monterey) 54
masons 62, 85
mayordomo 62, 66, 106
measles 65
merchants 55
Mexican War of Independence
    54
Michumash 24
Miguelito Canyon 57, 89
militia 15, 49, 67, 68
Mission Account Book 58, 59

missionaries 14, 20, 35, 37, 45, 46,
    47, 56, 63, 70, 80, 82, 83, 89,
    105, 106
missions 9, 13, 14, 15, 16, 18, 25, 32,
    34, 35, 40, 44, 47, 48, 52, 55,
    58, 60, 62, 65, 69, 76, 79, 80,
    82, 83, 84, 86, 87, 88, 89, 90
Mission San Buenaventura 18, 83
Mission San Luis Obispo 60, 76,
    107, 116
Mission Santa Bárbara 11, 49, 60,
    69, 75, 89, 124, 125
Mission Santa Inés 38, 48, 49, 50,
    67, 69, 70, 73, 85, 107
Mission Vieja 35, 37, 38, 40, 41,
    42, 52, 57, 89, 105
monjerio 64
Moreno, Father Juan 51, 84
music 34, 48
musicians 62, 86
musket 67, 70, 72, 76

N

National Park Service 88, 92, 93, 121
neophytes 9, 14, 15, 32, 38, 40, 44,
    45, 47, 49, 50, 53, 59, 62, 63,
    64, 65, 66, 67, 69, 74, 79, 83,
    84, 85, 109, 112
Neve, Governor Felipe de 18
Nocto 25
nurse 66

O

Obispeño 25, 32, 34
oil paintings 38
oleander 88
olive trees 89
Orámas, Father Cristóbal 45
orchard 40, 52, 53, 85, 89, 108
Ordáz, Father Blas 50, 69, 72, 73, 74

original plants 88, 123
Ortega, Corporal José Maria 37
Ortega, Francisco 54
Ortega, Juan 54
Ortega Rancho 67, 88, 124, 126
Ortegas 57, 65, 124
Osio, Antonio María (account of
    1824 revolt) 70, 77, 79
Oso Flaco 59, 76

P

Pacomio, José (Chumash revolt
    leader) 74, 79, 80, 83
paintings 34, 38, 40
paqwots 26, 34
Payeras, Father Mariano 40, 46,
    47, 48, 49, 50, 53, 54, 55, 57,
    59, 65, 68, 69, 107
pear tree 89
Pedernales 25, 57
Pico, Governor Pío 84, 86, 88, 124
pipe organs 86
Point Conception 17, 25, 58
Point Sal 25, 32, 117
pomegranates 89
Portolá, Captain Gaspar de 17,
    31, 116
poultry raisers 66
pozole 63
pozolera 64, 107
presidio of Loreto in Baja
    (supplied) 54
presidios 13, 47, 54, 55, 63, 79
Pueblo de la Purísima 83
pueblos 13, 47, 83
punishments 64
Purismeño 25, 31, 32, 34, 47, 83, 84

R

Rancho Reyes 57, 59, 107

ranchos 58, 81, 88
Rancho San Antonio 58, 59, 60,
    61, 107
Rancho San Julian 61
Rancho San Marcos 60
reatas 52
red maids 31
Refugio 60, 65, 67
Reyes, Antonio 54, 59
Reyes, Juan Francisco 59
Ripoll, Father Antonio 49
rituals, religious 34
Robinson, Alfred 58, 66, 83, 97
Rodríguez, Father Antonio 49, 50,
    72, 77, 78, 80
Rowe, Ed 88, 89, 123, 125

S

sacristan 66, 70, 78
Salsipuedes 57, 107
Salsipuedes Canyon 60, 89
San Antonio 58
San Antonio Creek 58, 61
San Antonio Valley 60
Sánchez, Father José 50
San Franciscita 58, 60
San Joaquin Valley 25, 47, 76
San Marcos Pass 37, 60, 89
San Pablo 58
Santa Bárbara Channel 17, 18, 24
Santa Inés 41, 46, 49, 56, 60, 69,
    70, 72, 74, 75, 87, 88
Santa Lucia 58, 60, 108
Santa Rosa 18, 24
Santa Ynez River 9, 17, 18, 40, 42,
    57, 58, 60, 61, 65, 67, 89, 107
Santa Ynez Valley 60
Sarría, Father Vicente 79
Saxpil 61
sea otter 55

seeds 13, 31, 63, 64, 125
Serra, Fray Junípero 18, 62
shamen 85
sheep 34, 40, 47, 53, 57, 58, 64
Shilimaqshtush 25, 31, 32
Shoy'ama, Pastor 85, 86
Shuman Canyon 59, 60
siliyik 25
singers 26, 48, 66, 86, 87
Sitio de Jalama 58
Sitio de Misión Vieja 58
skills 14, 62
smallpox 65, 84, 85
Solá, Governor Vicente de 67
soldados de cuera 54
soldiers 15, 35, 41, 64
specie in soap and tobaccco 54
State Highway 246 42
State Historic Park 7, 9, 11, 52, 58,
    90, 95
state of California 9, 87, 92, 94
Stations of the Cross 38
statues 34, 38
surpluses to newly founded
    missions 53
swivel guns 77

T

tallow 14, 53, 56, 57
Tapia, Corporal Tiburcio 72, 73, 113
Tápis, Father Estévan 47, 48, 58,
    59, 60
temescals 29
Temple, Juan 86
Todos Santos 58, 59
tomols 29
trades 16, 62, 84

U

Ulibarri, Father Francisco Román 49
Union Oil Company 87, 92
Uría, Father Francisco 46, 70, 72

V

Vallejo, General Mariano 80, 81
vaquero 15, 66, 68, 84, 102
Venansio, Indian musician 86
Ventureño 25
villages 15, 25, 26, 29, 32, 34, 35,
    44, 61, 64, 85, 116
vineyard 52, 57, 58, 60, 85, 87, 89
Vitoria, Father Marcos Antonio
    Salazar de 50, 83, 84
Vizcaíno, Sebastián 17

W

weapons 54, 72, 73, 79
weavers 62
Webb, Edith 93
wheat 40, 52, 58, 59, 64, 65
wheat rust 52
witch doctors 80
witnesses 66
wot 25

Z

Zanja de Cota 87

About the Author

M ichael Hardwick graduated from the University of California–Santa Barbara in 1972 with a degree in anthropology. While attending UCSB, Mike did early archaeology on the presidio in Santa Barbara, which is now a state historic park. He served on the Board of Directors of the Santa Barbara Trust for Historic Preservation for seventeen years. Michael is now an Honorary Life Trustee of the trust. His interest in Spanish colonial history spans forty-five years.

In the 1970s, Michael worked at La Purísima Mission State Historic Park and established an archive there. As a seasonal interpretive specialist in 1973, he produced a report entitled "La Purísima Mission State Historic Park Archives: An Experiment in Interpretation and Preservation." This was the beginning of an archives concept at La Purísima. The project was partially funded from a grant of the La Purísima Citizens Advisory Committee, which was still very active at the mission.

Michael Hardwick as an interpretive specialist at La Purísima Mission State Historic Park in the mission archives. Lompoc Record, *August 1972.*

Michael directed a staff of several seasonal employees to document, organize and register artifact collections, furnishings and historic property at the mission. The staff arranged historic correspondence, photographs and restoration blueprints and compiled mission garden information. Artifacts were used to develop historic themes.

From 1973 to 1980, Michael served as a state park ranger intermittent at La Purísima Mission State Historic Park. Subsequent to that, he became a docent at the mission after completing a ten-week training program in April 2002.

In 2005, Mike wrote his first book entitled *Changes in Landscape: The Beginnings of Horticulture in the California Missions.* In the spirit of the early horticultural work that was done for the restoration of Mission La Purísima, Michael's book identified much of the horticulture that was to be found at many of the early California missions. It became the basis for the Huerta Project at Old Mission Santa Bárbara. He was a founding member of that project, which preserves and propagates heritage plants of the California missions, as was done at Mission La Purísima.

The California Mission Studies Association awarded the 2015 CMSA President's Award to Michael Hardwick for his outstanding research of the Spanish missions and presidios in California.

www.ingramcontent.com/pod-product-compliance
Lightning Source LLC
Chambersburg PA
CBHW060807100426

42813CB00004B/973